A New Challenge for Western Europe

A VIEW FROM BONN

A NEW CHALLENGE FOR WESTERN EUROPE

A VIEW FROM BONN

WALTHER LEISLER KIEP

Foreword by GEORGE W. BALL

 Mason & Lipscomb PUBLISHERS   NEW YORK

COPYRIGHT © 1974 *by Walther Leisler Kiep*

English translation first published in U.S.A.
by Mason & Lipscomb, Publishers, Inc., New York, in 1974.
Original German edition copyright © Seewald Verlag, Dr. Heinrich
Seewald, Stuttgart 1972

All rights reserved

No part of this book may be reproduced in any form
without permission in writing from the publisher

FIRST PRINTING

ISBN: 0-88405-053-X

Library of Congress Catalog Card Number: 73-92441

Printed in the United States of America

Contents

Author's Note   vii

Foreword by George W. Ball   ix

1.
The Renaissance of the International Scene   1

2.
America's View of Itself As a World Power   13

3.
America's New Role As a World Power   27

4.
Americans and Russians at the Negotiating Table   49

5.
The New Partnership with Europe   61

6.
The Crisis of American Society   77

7.
The Role of West Germany
As a Medium-Sized Power   85

8.
The German-American Alliance   111

9.
Conflict and Consensus in the Third Postwar
Decade   125

10.
Anti-Americanism in West Germany   135

11.
The Politics of Détente in Europe   143

12.
New Forms of Nuclear Partnership   163

13.
The Monetary Crisis in International Affairs   183

14.
From the Industrial to the Post-Industrial
Society   205

Acknowledgments   219

Author's Note

A new strategy of détente and cooperation between world powers is taking shape against the geopolitical skyline. Its outline, increasingly defined as major shifts in power alliances solidify, casts a shadow across the Western Alliance. The economic and military security enjoyed by the United States and its allies, the medium-sized nations of Western Europe, has fostered an attitude of complacency—a dangerous stance given the insecure and questionable nature of the American presence in Europe since Vietnam. To counter the agressive tactics of the Soviet Union in its drive for hegemony in Europe, and in the interest of worldwide détente, efforts should now be stepped up to bring about the political unification of Western Europe. With the development of this new arm of world power, a much-needed "politics of the West" will grow, resulting in a modus for cooperation among Western nations.

WALTHER LEISLER KIEP

Bonn
September 1973

Foreword

Since every nation approaches the formulation of its own foreign policy in pre-Copernican terms—as though it were the center of the cosmos—we Americans should find it a humbling and useful experience to examine the questions that currently preoccupy us—*détente*, the state of the Western Alliance, relations with the Soviet Union, Japan and China—from a point of vantage other than Washington. As one discovers on looking through a stereoscope the observation of the same object—or, in this case the same subject—from different points in space provides a depth and definition that can greatly increase the viewer's perception.

In this book, Walther Kiep makes that possible for us. Because he explicitly offers "a view from Bonn" rather than from Washington, his perceptions may seem to us slightly out of focus, with nuances of shading and emphasis with which we are not fully familiar. Yet it is these differences that give the American edition of the book a special utility.

What Walther Kiep has written is no speculative essay but the comments of a practising German politician, a leader of the CDU and a man of influence within his own party. The fact that he has sketched his views with such candor and clarity is one more piece of evidence that the Federal Republic has finally come of age. It has outgrown its inhibitions against an assertive and independent foreign policy and is seeking to carve out a national role consistent with its own traditions and personality yet within the framework of close understanding between Bonn and Washington. Walther Kiep is emphatic and unambiguous on the need for a continuing close relation between West Germany and the United States—a relation that amounts, as he describes it, to "a second constitution for West Germany"—for America's nuclear umbrella is, as he sees it, the Federal Republic's sole guarantee that it will not slip into the Soviet sphere of influence.

It is because Mr. Kiep places such emphasis on relations between the Federal Republic and the United States that he is necessarily disturbed by recent developments that cast doubt on America's course in the future. What his book clearly discloses is how the ambiguities of American policy have disturbed our closest friends abroad.

The basic confusion derives from the difference between what the United States has said and what it has, in fact, done. The process began in the summer of 1969, with the so-called Nixon Doctrine, which announced, in effect, that the United States would no longer assume responsibilities all over the world but would leave more and more problems to be solved by local effort. Though this doctrine was intended primarily for Asia and not for Europe, the distinction was never made explicit.

What many Europeans feared was that the United States would consciously diminish its world role, sinking back into a traditional isolationism. What, in fact, the

Nixon Administration has done, however, is greatly to increase the scope and pace of America's diplomatic activities through a series of initiatives directed primarily at the major Communist powers.

Only slowly are the Europeans beginning to understand that what the Nixon Doctrine really intended was less to signal a diminution in America's world role than to gain freedom of maneuver for unilateral initiatives. Adding to the confusion, of course, has been the endless speculation about multi-polarity and particularly the President's ill-advised talk about "five balancing powers" which implied an abandonment of alliance diplomacy. Unhappily, an addiction to unilateralism is a habit on which the current American Administration is securely hooked, since it is integrally related to the Nixon-Kissinger diplomatic style. Adapted—deliberately or subconsciously—from General de Gaulle, who raised it to a highly polished art form, that style consists of identifiable components: use of dazzling surprise announcements to keep the world—including the domestic opposition—off balance; an elaborate exploitation of the theatricals of summitry; the personalization of diplomacy by emphasis on the individual *tour de force* thus reducing relations between nations to a kind of trial by combat between illustrious champions; and the reduction of the established apparatus of foreign policy, embassies and foreign offices, to subordinate and largely administrative roles.

We have seen the fruits of the unilateralism that goes hand in hand with such individualistic diplomacy in Europe's chilly response to Mr. Kissinger's well-intended but belated efforts to reassure our allies with slogans and symbols, such as the "Year of Europe" and the "new Atlantic Charter." Yet, so long as America remains under its present leadership, there seems little chance of change. In spite of Mr. Kissinger's often avowed intention to return to an "institutionalized" diplomacy (in which he no doubt intellectually believes) it is not yet demonstrated that he has the temperament for a more traditional practice. That doubt, long present, has been strongly reenforced by his single-handed effort to resolve the Middle Eastern predicament by frenetic jet travel.

It is no wonder, therefore, that Mr. Kiep is confused and disturbed by America's activities in Moscow and Peking and the loose talk of *détente* it engenders. Contrary to most Europeans, for whom Japanese concerns are totally uninteresting, he sees a clear parallel between Japan's anxieties concerning the United States' relations with China and the Federal Republic's anxieties with regard to our own relations with the Soviet Union. Both Japan and the Federal Republic live under the American nuclear umbrella, and in each case these new relations raise questions as to the reliability of the American nuclear commitment.

It is largely for this reason that he puts such emphasis on the maintenance of American troop deployments in Germany as a visible and tangible evidence of America's continuing determination to defend Europe.

Contrary to many Europeans, Mr. Kiep is not led astray by talk of *détente*. He recognizes that this vague ill-defined state of affairs has meant for the Soviet Union merely a change of tactics and not of long-run strategic objectives, and he sees in Moscow's employment of the politics of *détente* an effort to push the United States out of its European involvement, while at the same time luring the Federal Republic away from the Western alliance.

As a German, Mr. Kiep cannot help but call attention to the brooding problem of reunification, but he is not so obsessed with it as to let it obscure the Federal Republic's need to recognize its identity and responsibilities as a major nation-state rather than remain paralyzed either by past memories or deferred hopes.

Thus, unlike many in his own party, Mr. Kiep supports the *Ostpolitik* as a pragmatic measure needed to provide a sense of permanence to a Federal Republic that postwar Germans had been taught to regard as provisional, so as to give it the confidence to play an effective role in the larger world politics. Yet he believes that the bilateral phase of the *Ostpolitik* has now ended and that from now on the Federal Republic must pursue that policy in a multilateral setting. This is an important point, since to many Americans the dangers perceived in the *Ostpolitik* have derived not merely from the fear of the euphoria that it might engender but from the example it might provide to other smaller European states, leading them to try to make their own peace with Moscow from a position of weakness.

Some of his countrymen have had difficulty reconciling the *Ostpolitik* with the postwar drive toward the unity of Western Europe. After all the competing seductions of an *Ostpolitik* and a *Westpolitik*—the need to choose between an East-looking and a West-looking policy—have haunted German politics for almost two centuries. More often than not Germans have resolved the argument by turning Eastward.

But, though recognizing the dangerous attractions of an Eastern adventure, particularly for the leftward leaning members of the new generation, he seems confident that his country can contain the aberrant potentials of its *Ostpolitik*. What is needed is to give renewed vitality to the two principal counter-forces: close ties with the United States (assuring nuclear protection) and —equally important—European progress not only toward economic integration but political unity. Here he sees the recent entry of Britain into the European Community as offering a basis for a European *relancement.*

But, though European unity is clearly the hope of the future, it is not the present reality. In spite of brave words and the dedication of able and serious men, Europe is not now, and—even on the happiest assumptions—will not be for many years, a unified political entity, capable of formulating a common foreign policy or of making prompt and clean-cut decisions on any major political issue. Retarded by years of Gaullist obstructionism, it is at best in an early stage of political consciousness. It cannot make political moves outside its own regional sphere; the most it can do is to respond sluggishly to American initiatives with a painfully negotiated and heavily compromised position that represents the lowest common denominator of the policies and politics of its component states.

The awkwardness implicit in such a transitional situation is, at the moment, an abrasive element in trans-Atlantic relations, leading to considerable pettishness among technocrats on both sides of the ocean. Yet that may be only a foreshadowing of more serious substantive disputes to come, as Europe achieves a greater political reality. Ever since the Administration of President Eisenhower America has, as a matter of national policy, encouraged the development of a Europe that could speak with one voice and act with a single will. At the same time many Europeans have embraced that cause primarily as a means of gaining independence from the United States, so that Europe could hold its own in an Atlantic partnership. The two ideas are by no means incompatible since any American who has thought seriously about the problem must recognize that just as European integration will inevitably make Europe a more effective commercial competitor, so political unity will make it, to some extent, a rival in the development of world policies. In the long run such a situation cannot help but be healthy, because, just as commercial rivalry encourages efficiency and stimulates effort, so competition in the market place of political ideas and actions should produce sounder policies. America, after all, has no monopoly of political wisdom nor any immunity from political error, as we spectacularly demonstrated in Viet Nam.

There are compelling reasons why this situation should be accepted with understanding and a resolute patience on the part of Americans, since Europe's progress toward unity, halting though it may be, is, in a very real sense, the fulfillment of a long-standing American objective. Nevertheless events have now shown with painful vividness that the idea of European nations acting together and not automatically applauding every American move is irksome to an American Administration which has, from the beginning, had a greater intellectual affinity for Gaullism than for a politically united Europe—an Administration that delights in the hatching of new initiatives through secret diplomacy which it then unveils with a flamboyance reminiscent of the opening of a new Hollywood theater in the 1950s.

Thus one cannot dismiss the possibility that the awkward transition period Europe is now experiencing may produce misunderstandings and disenchantment that can seriously fray the bonds of mutual interest which have given cohesion to our Atlantic relations during the whole postwar period.

Nor is it likely, on the other hand, that anti-Americanism will spur Europe toward the achievement of a greater unity. It has long been a poignant hope on the part of some Good Europeans that, if America were to grow impatient with Europe's plodding progress, Europe would be goaded to faster action by the desire to meet America on its own terms. Yet that seems to me a vain conceit; I do not see America playing the classic role of unifying state by serving as a common enemy. Though the United States may annoy Europeans it will never terrify them and the existence of a disaffected America is more likely to incite fragmentation than encourage unity.

Thus Europeans are going to have to find their own way, guided by an increasing comprehension that only by unifying can the European peoples ever make a contribution to the world commensurate with their traditions, their material resources and their precious qualities of spirit and intellect.

In that effort Germany must of necessity play a leading role.

GEORGE W. BALL

A New Challenge for Western Europe
A VIEW FROM BONN

1

The Renaissance of the International Scene

International politics is dead! Long live international politics!

The beginning of the seventies saw the outbreak of a wave of diplomatic travel by world leaders, the likes of which has never been seen before. It was almost like a chess game. The most spectacular journey was that made by President Nixon. Without doubt, his trip to Peking will be seen as an historic turning point in the evolution of international politics. But travel by prominent figures in world affairs has been by no means a diplomatic tactic used only by the Americans. After their long self-imposed exile from the international scene, the Chinese themselves rediscovered the world through travel. They took their seat in the United Nations and dispatched large delegations to countries around the globe. Their visit to France aroused a particular sensation in Europe.

And since it is almost a truism that wherever China is busy, Japan cannot be far behind, Emperor Hirohito's tour through many of the European countries also reminded the world that Japan is very much alive and well and in a position to play a role in world politics.

For their part, the rulers of the Kremlin unleashed

2] A New Challenge for Western Europe

a veritable flood of diplomatic travelers—Brezhnev, Podgorny, and Kosygin.

West Germany also contributed to the international travel season. Brandt's trip to the Crimea left its own impact on the international community. It inspired the sort of speculation that arises when a neighbor of moderate means suddenly embarks on a world cruise after previously limiting himself to brief outings in the countryside.

Is all this high-level international travel-cum-diplomacy a new style in foreign relations, or merely an ongoing aspect of processes long underway? A major factor is today's jet transportation which makes possible visits among world leaders within a matter of hours. More important, the need of the world's top political figures to speak directly with one another rather than through emissaries has become increasingly desirable in the postwar era. Since World War II, nations have become more interdependent, and their problems even more interrelated. Because of this, there is no longer a clear-cut distinction between what used to be purely a domestic issue and a foreign policy issue. The lines have blurred. Thus, the trend towards a kind of domestic politics of the world almost seems to make it imperative that the leading statesmen gather information at firsthand.

There is nothing new in statesmen traveling to enhance their domestic political images. Leaders have been doing it for years. British Prime Ministers have made a regular habit of scheduling conferences with foreign leaders on the eve of new elections. In West Germany it has been the norm to visit the United States before elections. Chancellor Konrad Adenauer himself set the precedent for this approach with his trip to the

United States in 1953. American Presidential candidates seem to have made foreign travel a prerequisite to campaigning.

But summitry as a tool of diplomacy fell somewhat into disuse following the debacle of the Eisenhower-Khrushchev meeting in Paris in 1960. Now it has been revived, and there seems to be a new kind of urgency propelling these diplomatic travelers across borders.

The early seventies have witnessed such unprecedented political tourism that future historians may well point to it as a period of revolution in the international system. We are clearly witnessing a rebirth of international politics. It was only a few years ago that we observed among nations a general retreat from foreign affairs in favor of domestic issues. Confronted with student unrest, the emerging problems of industrialized society such as environmental pollution and violent crime, and the necessity for broad social reform, nations assigned a low priority to foreign affairs in order to devote themselves to higher-priority domestic problems.

But new pressures generated by world politics have compelled politicians to concentrate on foreign policy. Foreign policy and domestic policy cannot be compartmentalized. It is like playing with a keyboard. Push one button down, and another button jumps up. That is the way foreign policy and domestic policy work in an interrelated world. An action that one country takes affects other countries. No country can go it alone in this day and age.

Is a renewed preeminence of foreign over domestic affairs evidenced here? The practical politician does not see this distinction. Foreign policy, commonly viewed as an effort to improve a nation's position in the world, today involves primarily the promotion of national security and economic strength. These concerns are basic complements to all domestic policy. One has only to consider the role of international trade in an industrial nation like West Germany to realize the interdependence of domestic and foreign policies. Its domestic economy depends to a great degree on its success in international trade, and the government services it can provide depend to a great extent on the vigor of its domestic economy.

Brandt is one example of many statesmen who have wished to devote themselves to the domestic sphere but who have instead had to concentrate on foreign affairs. He wanted to be the Chancellor of domestic reform. He became the Chancellor of *Ostpolitik* (Eastern policy, specifically encompassing the Soviet Union and the other Communist countries of Eastern Europe). The same situation has applied to the leading politicians of the world powers. The Russians hoped to compete with and equal the Americans in raising the Soviet standard of living. The Americans hoped to reconcile the many camps into which American society had divided itself. China promoted its cultural revolution to renew and maintain a revolutionary spirit judged to be in danger of extinction. Yet, without having resolved their domestic problems, all these nations were forced to concentrate on foreign affairs.

Naturally, the suspicion arises that statesmen may have fled from their pressing domestic burdens to world affairs because they could address themselves to this arena with greater prospects for prestige and success. But this would be to oversimplify the new international situation. This situation has shown that only a few nations can indulge in the sort of classical neutrality the Swedes and Swiss enjoy. West Germany is locked into world politics, above all, through its alliance with the United States. It can no more pretend to be Switzerland than can the United States pretend to be Sweden. If the survival and further development of the social order represent the primary goals underlying the politics of all nations, these goals can only be achieved through a coordination of domestic and foreign affairs. The vital element tying the two fields together is money. The British Conservative Reginald Maudling put the problem in these terms: "The decisive question is not how much money we have to protect our country, but how much money do we need for its security?" To evaluate this question as realistically as possible today requires worldwide diplomacy and as sober an assessment of international politics as possible. Only the politician who is able to do this may venture to distinguish between the political priorities of international security and domestic needs. The search for some form of international détente is paralleled by a concern that funds be available to promote the adaptability of domestic societies to their current and future needs. So, foreign policy is in the fashion once again. But it is more than just a passing fad.

Tripolar Prospects

The world political scene is changing. New incentives for initiatives in foreign affairs exist not only for the superpowers but for medium and small nations as well. A glance at West Germany's foreign policy program shows these changes. Ostpolitik, the expansion of the Common Market, and the crisis of the international monetary system are three problem areas West Germany is attempting to come to grips with simultaneously. International politics is in a state of flux. Nations compete in a sort of foreign affairs Olympics, each trying for the gold medal. As President Nixon stated in a report to Congress: "This administration has to lead the nation through a period of fundamental changes in international affairs."

This transformation is under way below the level of the world politics that are still determined by the two superpowers, the Soviet Union and the United States. On their level, the superpowers are anxious to maintain the military balance between them and to avoid any substantial shift of power. Confronting each other with the most modern weaponry, they bear responsibility for the very survival of human existence. Nothing has altered this reality and, for the time being, nothing will. Militarily, the world remains characterized by true confrontation between the two poles of the United States and the Soviet Union. Yet this nuclear bipolarity has not prevented the development of a political multipolarity, and does not rule out the rise of a third world power.

The triangle of the United States, the Soviet Union, and China is the distinguishing feature of the shift under way in world politics. The triangle is not yet equilateral; China clearly remains as the shortest side. Yet, as the scene of world politics shifts from Europe to Asia, the Chinese have every chance of assuming a full and equal place among the world powers. In fact, the existence of this prospect is a realization that has become increasingly clear to the Germans: the center of gravity in international politics is shifting from the Atlantic Ocean to the Pacific. Europe and European questions will no longer determine the course and climate of world affairs.

There is every indication that the problems of Asia will set the tempo for future developments on the world stage. From the points of view of Germany and Europe, this is not a comfortable trend.

Looking at this international political triangle, one sees first of all that Moscow and Washington continue to concern themselves with global problems as they have in the past. Which will be the leading power in the world? In Europe? In the Middle East? And in Vietnam and Asia? That is the question. Between Moscow and Peking, on the other hand, the main issue is the leadership position in the Communist camp. The motives for this case lie not so much in ideological differences as in the political rivalry for influence in Asia. The fact that the Soviet Union and China have a long border in common, which is disputed between them, intensifies the conflict. Chou En-lai revealed in an interview that the Chinese even anticipate a Soviet nuclear attack. As a result, most of the major and middle-sized cities of the People's Republic have networks of underground shelters. Today it seems that in the long run the Russians have greater fear of the Chinese than of the Europeans, and the Chinese are uncertain whether they should have greater fear of Russia or Japan. For the moment, the Chinese take to the field against that "established revolutionary power, the Soviet Union" and inveigh against the "imperialism" of the United States.

Only a decade ago, when the first feelers were being sent out to China, Nixon, the politician, warned against admitting Red China to the United Nations. In his view, by doing such a thing, countries that wanted peace and freedom in the world would only make themselves appear "ridiculous" by considering Red China as a "peace-loving" member of the world community. As

President of the United States, the same man has seen the opening of contacts with the People's Republic as essential. Obviously, one's view of a particular situation depends on where one sits.

Yet America's main concern in Asia is the containment of China. Thus, another aspect of American Asian policy will be how to prevent China from entering the vacuum that the current American withdrawal in Asia leaves behind. Finally, it is a matter of concern to the two superpowers, America and Russia, that China be kept from breaking the nuclear stalemate in some way. The American attempt to develop new politics with China has been supported substantially through the ambiguity of Soviet reactions. Not only did the Soviet Union fail to develop a clear position vis-à-vis the West, but it also has spent years without being able to settle on a modus vivendi with China. This, too, is a part of the new triangular configuration in world politics.

It is often extraordinarily difficult for observers to anticipate future developments or even to explain the present relations between Russia and China. In these two countries, the motivations behind political actions are anxiously hidden from the outside world. Furthermore, in both countries developments in international politics are only hesitantly recognized because the leaders have attempted to protect their countries from outside influences. International strategy in the case of either country, however, is by no means immune to unexpected changes, abrupt breaks, or constant variations. All experts on both Soviet and Chinese politics therefore must still, it seems, include in their bag of analytical tricks the fine art of interpreting tea leaves and crystal-ball-gazing.

Are three world powers as many as there will ever

be? In October, 1971, Theo Sommer, political editor of the German weekly paper, *Die Zeit,* dared to prognosticate in an article on world politics. "The world of 1980 or perhaps even that of 1975 will be pentapolar, not tripolar." In such a world, statesmen will be practicing a diplomatic craft à la Bismarck, trying to juggle five balls instead of the present two. China's involvement in international politics already represents the awakening of one sleeping giant. In the postwar period, Japan limited itself to reconstruction in a manner similar to West Germany. Today it, too, has political interests to pursue more aggressively than in the past. Like Japan, finally, a united Western Europe would have the potential of becoming a world power. The appearance of such a Europe on the international scene would lead to substantial changes—an easing of the burdens now carried by the United States and an end to the increasing transfer of focus in international affairs to the Asian area.

And the Third World? The number of countries in this category has almost tripled. This change is evidenced in the membership roster of the United Nations. The Third World countries made a substantial contribution to the defeat of the United States in the vote by which Chiang's China was traded for Mao's China in the U.N. But the excitement of the Third World countries over the result of that vote must not obscure the fact that in their exclusion of Taiwan they have provided an example themselves of how small countries are dealt with today. Their influence is clearly on the decline. Only ten years ago, the leaders of the Third World—Nehru, Sukarno, Ben Bella, Nkrumah, and Nasser—made daily headlines in the world press. Today the problems of the Third World have been pushed into the background. Has the reorientation of the great industrial nations to their own problems and their new international political undertakings finally forced the developing countries off the map of world politics? Have they become merely a by-product of the new international politics?

It is hardly possible to assume that the gap between the poor and the rich in the measurement of the nations of the globe can play an inferior role for very long. It is much more likely that this conflict will push its way into the foreground soon again and contribute to world politics once more. The People's Republic of China could well come to be a new leading spokesman for the Third World. But there is also the possibility that the highly industrialized nations, Japan on one side of the world and Western Europe on the other, might hurry to the aid of developing countries. Whether the changes under way in current world politics will be continuous or merely a path to the consolidation of a new phase will be decided in the international handling of the problems of the developing countries.

The Prospects of the Medium-Sized Powers

Two typical representatives of the medium powers in the future will be the nuclear powers, Great Britain and France, but the role of these two countries in world politics can hardly be based on their nuclear arsenals any longer. In this day of antiballistic missiles, the international balance of power is not at all susceptible to influence through their limited nuclear weapons systems. In terms of world politics, the future of Great Britain and France lies only in a united Europe.

It has now become possible for the medium-sized states to undertake their own initiatives in world politics once again. But the gap, in terms of real military power between the medium-sized states and the superpowers, America and the Soviet Union, is growing. It remains to be seen what potential China can develop. For the time being, the United States and the Soviet Union will continue to span the international system with their bipolar responsibility. But since the use of the nuclear capacities of these powers is becoming increasingly unlikely in view of the enormous destruction potential of these weapons, the nuclear stalemate offers opportunities for the medium-sized powers to play a more important role. The same process is also naturally stimulated to the extent the two nuclear powers work together. In fact, this is the peculiarity of the shared American-Soviet nuclear responsibility today. Their relations are characterized by a juxtaposition of both cooperation and confrontation.

For the individual states of the world, as for example West Germany, it becomes vital to know in which areas the relations of the superpowers are ones of cooperation and which are ones of confrontation. A cooperative phase seems to be taking form in Europe at the moment because in that region confrontation could still quickly reach the threshold of nuclear war.

In the future, there is no doubt that the Soviet Union will continue to strive to pursue a foreign policy of expansion. It will continue to attempt to take advantage of every hotbed of unrest and every power vacuum in the world to its own benefit. It has not by far given up its aim to advance against the West. Naturally, the later Stalinist "heave-ho" methods in foreign policy have been moderated in the meantime through an explicit element of caution.

The tensions between a political multipolarity and

a military bipolarity of the superpowers are reflected in alliances, such as West Germany's with the United States. Apart from a few separate agreements, the main provisions of our alliance with the United States are contained in treaties concluded in a multilateral framework. This German-American alliance is a given constant in the dynamics of current international politics. As the leading power of the Western world, the United States is unavoidably tied to the changing scene in international politics in all of its aspects. For this reason, it is important to take a careful look at the situation of the United States and the developments that are under way.

2

America's View of Itself
As a World Power

Before we can analyze the forces of international politics that affect current political thinking in the United States, we must concern ourselves with the key problem that dominated all political consideration of America for so long: Vietnam. The failure of the American involvement in Vietnam can lead only to the conclusion that a superpower cannot necessarily achieve a victory against a substantially weaker enemy at any price. Even the "peace with honor" result cannot obscure the fact that the United States came out of the Vietnam war with less credibility as an international leader, uncertain of its international commitments, and questioning long-accepted moral standards. At this point, it is not unreasonable to assume that a kind of "Vietnam complex" that has built up in the American character will have a deep psychological impact on the foreign—and domestic—policy of the United States in the coming decade.

As a result of Vietnam, escalation became a fashionable word. It was used to describe the development of the American involvement in the Vietnam war. It characterized the step-by-step entanglement in the conflict which began through the deployment of military advisers and ended with a long and almost all-out war. In retrospect it is clear that the United States had neither a strategic concept in mind nor did it know politically or militarily exactly what it wanted. The "Pentagon Papers"—extracts from high-level memoranda, staff minutes, and other materials which gave a clue to the American government's decision-making processes concerning Vietnam—give some impressions of this confused history. It is true these do not represent an historical documentation sufficient to explain clearly the how and why of American involvement in the Vietnam war. But they do give an impression of how a world power can stumble into such a conflict more or less by accident.

It is from this kind of situation that America's Vietnam complex has developed. The United States recognized that it could not finish off the conflict it had taken on. At the same time, the country began to doubt its own capabilities as a world leader. The American superpower had undertaken to prove in Vietnam that it could easily quell the guerrilla war which the Communists had provoked. But conditions in Vietnam were in fact so unfavorable that public opinion around the world could conclude only the opposite: Superpowers are not at all in a position to deal with guerrilla wars.

Strategically, American action in Vietnam was based on the so-called "domino theory," developed during the Eisenhower years. If Indochina were to fall into the hands of the Communists, Burma, Thailand, Malaysia and Indonesia would follow, falling like dominoes one after another in a line. Then countries like Japan and the Philippines, and even Australia and New Zealand would be in danger. Consequently, it would become impossible to contain the influence of China as the leading power of Asia.

In the last analysis then, the involvement of the

United States in Vietnam was an attempt to rule out Chinese hegemony in Asia. This prospect could only be achieved if the domestic politics of the states to be protected could be consolidated. But this goal contained the great weak point of the "foreign policy shorthand" involved in the domino theory. The United States allied itself with states whose domestic problems resisted solution and which were too weak to deal with them on their own. The result was that world opinion soon began to condemn the United States involvement, because it was not clear that America was pursuing the interests of the people for whom it was intervening.

Thus, questions were raised as to the political and moral objectives behind the American policies. Was the country's involvement in Vietnam really a stand for the ideas of democracy and liberalism against dictatorial Communist ideology? This question was discussed controversially above all in the United States itself. Criticism of the war in Vietnam was a substantial impulse behind the rebellion of America's young people. But it did not remain limited to these circles alone. The horror of the war came to the attention of all Americans every day. No war was ever so heavily reported. Americans saw it every day on television. Instances involving American soldiers were cited as war crimes. Finally, it came out that a large number of American soldiers in Vietnam had become narcotics addicts. International political considerations aside, the Vietnam question became a human question for America's citizens, and it culminated in the demand: "Bring the boys home." This desire to pull American soldiers out of a meaningless, unwinnable, and brutal war represented the decisive breakthrough in the domestic politics that led to withdrawal from Vietnam.

The war in Vietnam became a trauma for American society. The emotions it aroused are comparable only to those stimulated by the Civil War, which was the most devastating experience America had ever known. The war in Vietnam led to a reconsideration of the goals, the moral standards, and even the whole way of life of the United States. Americans also became more sensitive to the criticism that made its way to them from foreign countries concerning the Vietnam debacle. Even those Americans who had criticized the war themselves were struck by the firmness and the animosity towards the United States with which the war was condemned around the world, particularly among their allies and among neutral countries. America's failure gave the country its first real taste of world condemnation.

It is no surprise then that the United States is now involved in a reconsideration of its relations to the world environment. The heart of this process is how entanglements à la Vietnam can be avoided in the future.

A Reassessment of Alliances

The United States has come out of the Vietnam conflict as a world power uncertain of its alliance commitments. A good question is whether Americans will be satisfied to limit themselves to a reconsideration of their activities up to this point alone. Will they now merely be more careful to avoid committing themselves so strongly in the world and making new alliances, or will this process lead to a radical break in existing alliance relations? Parallel to its reconsideration of existing commitments, the United States undertook a major effort to come to new terms with its most immediate antagonists, the Soviet Union and China. Are we witnessing a new weakness in the American superpower, manifest in that country's feeling obliged to negotiate with its leading rivals? Or is it a question of a new American approach to international politics, geared to a more radical pursuit of the nation's security and international political interests free from alliance politics and ideological considerations? Perhaps the alliance system approach of the United States up to this point was more or less an indirect strategy to avoid conflicts with its major rivals. After Vietnam, American foreign policy seems to be oriented towards a direct strategy of negotiation with these antagonists in search of lessening the threats to international security.

America's new uncertainty with regard to its alliances is of vital significance to the European nations. They fear a new American egocentrism. American involvement in Vietnam was based on the provisions of various alliances, especially SEATO. In this case, as in the case of the NATO alliance, an attack on one member is to be considered by other members as an attack on their own nations. These alliances were meant to guarantee the security of the areas involved in the name of freedom. Both NATO and America's commitment in Asia derived from the same spirit of resistance to Communism engendered in the era of Secretary of State John Foster Dulles.

In the near future, European statesmen will be obliged to formulate new arguments and provisions for the maintenance of the European-American alliance free from any shadow of the Vietnam trauma. In the same context, we shall have to reconsider what contribution we are ready to make to a defense against the Communist threat and just what the basis of Western defense preparedness can be.

The military service of the younger generation of voters on the political scene today represents the main source of our contribution to national defense. In a way, Vietnam was the introduction of this younger generation to current international politics.

Not only American but also European youth experienced a startling disillusionment as a result of the Vietnam conflict. The soundness of the concept of military service has been widely questioned. "Something is cracking in the branch our security force is sitting on. If the former snaps, the latter will fall." With this sentence, the German journalist, Bruno Dechamps, described the situation quite accurately. It will be a task for politics in the West to redefine the issues of defense preparedness within realistic limits. Even though Vietnam did not directly involve the European-American alliance, it nevertheless raised questions concerning the basis of the alliance in decisive new terms. We must ask and answer the common questions of whether and how we want to defend the freedom of the West against Communist dictatorship.

America's Old Ambition: To Provide an Example and Maintain Neutrality

America feels overburdened by its role in world affairs, and it has begun to reflect on its own condition. The process is in full gear in the Nixon administration. It determines the form of international politics today, and its result may produce a new international political constellation.

The history of the United States seems to be characterized by a basic discontent by the Americans of the American role in the realm of world politics. Some of this attitude may stem in part from the admonition issued by America's first president, George Washington, in his Farewell Address: "It is our policy to steer clear of permanent alliances with any portion of the foreign world." Contemporary discussion of neo-isolationism in the United States suggests a revival of the old bias by which foreign affairs are seen as an unnecessary burden. Certainly with regard to political skills and capabilities, the forte of the Americans lies less in international politics than in domestic affairs. The Americans did not discover the art of diplomacy, nor have they contributed in any substantial way to its historical development, even though their domestic political life has provided a whole set of exemplary developments. Generally one has the feeling that Americans are extraordinarily steady in their domestic situation.

Despite the United States' lack of concentration on diplomacy, American thinkers have had a major influence on the theories of international politics in our time. Since World War II, American statesmen have developed and applied American foreign policy from the format of concepts which the theorists have provided. Consideration of contemporary world conditions receives important impulses from America. The present Secretary of State, Henry Kissinger, is an example of the breed of engaged political thinkers who have often received opportunities to put their theories into international practice. A similar opportunity exists for those who have prepared themselves intensively in Asian studies, particularly in the study of China. The United States was not obliged to initiate its new relations with China in the dark, but was in a position to approach this political task with teams that were prepared in advance. In this quasi-academic context, we can still see the resources of the American society and its characteristically unqualified vitality. Political scientists in the United States have made a substantial contribution to the analysis of international politics. The names of Karl Deutsch, Stanley Hoffmann, and Hans J. Morgenthau—all academicians specializing in international affairs—come to mind, along with many others. Initiating whole schools of thought geared to international politics, these men have been devoted to an examination of new strategic world conditions.

The weakness—as well as the strength—of American foreign policy lies more in its institutions. It is difficult to maintain continuity in the policies of the United States in view of the frequently changing teams working with any given president. One positive aspect of American society is the circulation of people in the leadership positions. Scientists and businessmen go into political work and return after awhile to their original fields. At the same time, this process leads to a weakness in the institutions dealing with American foreign policy. The people change too often and too quickly. Almost two thousand positions have new occupants with any new President. An intellectual readiness for renewal and change has been affiliated with such turnovers. On the other hand, the pronounced lack of continuity in foreign policy offices has had a detrimental effect on the involvement of the Americans in international politics in the long run.

A critical question faces the Americans with regard to their foreign policy system: Can they really allow all basic questions to depend on one man—the President of the United States—to the extent they still commonly are? It should be noted, incidentally, that continuity in personnel related to foreign policy decisions is maintained in a general sense in the military sphere as well as in the career foreign service.

Americans have historically maintained two basic attitudes in their approach to foreign politics: They have wanted to provide a leading example to other nations, and they have wanted to maintain neutrality in international conflicts. Since the founding of the United States, Americans have believed in the international power of persuasion of their social and political system. They hoped to be effective through their good example alone. Their major antagonist, the Soviet Union, claims to gain its policy impulse through its world revolutionary mandate. By contrast, the Americans have wanted to rely completely on the attractiveness of their own example. One of the causes of their current uncertainties lies in their own growing doubt in the persuasiveness of this example. Americans from Benjamin Franklin to John F. Kennedy believed in the potential of their international missionary effort. The new doubt has been evidenced in the Johnson and Nixon administrations. Franklin spoke of the American spirit which was to be championed in the interest of the whole of humanity. The Americans had long played an active role in the international politics of the postwar years when Kennedy declared: "The United States has always represented the hope of the peoples of the world. I hope that in the future as well they will continue to show leadership and vision that can offer hope to the world."

However one judges the postwar involvement of the United States in international affairs, its global role would be inconceivable apart from the idealistic energy and zeal of the Americans and their belief in their democratic mission. That magnate of public opinion, Henry R. Luce, saw the advent of the "American century" in 1941. The United States was to be the dynamic heart of a new world and a "center of education for hardworking servants of democracy." Surely the postwar international involvement of the United States was based on far more substantial grounds than these. Nevertheless, the consensus on the world role of the United States even among Americans was seen largely in the basic sense of Luce's formulation.

To exaggerate only somewhat, one could say that Americans have only found their international role agreeable to the extent that it has been decked out in the missionary robes of idealistic motives. One may doubt that these motives have been the only ones involved, but their existence was in evidence again and again in the postwar relations between Germany and the United States.

Americans understood the prospect of providing a world example mainly in terms of a foreign policy of isolationism. As a basic rule for international politics, George Washington recommended the broadest possible development of economic ties with foreign states, but the most limited political ties. This has become the classic argument for American neutrality. In fact, until the end of the last century, the neutrality of the United States represented a steady factor in international politics. Even at the outbreak of World War I, President Wilson declared: "America must remain neutral in word and deed." But when the country went to war after all, it did so in a manner which has continued to characterize American foreign policy to this day. Stanley Hoffman has referred to this style as an indicative of the "Wilson syndrome": the tendency to see the tasks of the United

States in international politics in terms of moral and idealistic considerations. American disillusionment at the end of World War I followed from this American attitude towards foreign affairs. A new period of isolationism followed. Had it not been for this retreat into isolationism, the United States, working with the community of nations, might have been able to contribute to a lessening of the tensions that in the end led to World War II. But domestic problems, particularly in the economic sector of America, also contributed significantly to the mood.

This basic predisposition towards neutrality is further documented in a clear and practical preference among Americans for domestic politics. The United States was founded through the emigration of Europeans who wanted to live a new life in their own way under new circumstances. The clear primacy of domestic politics in the United States is derived from this aspiration to develop and participate in an independent political system isolated from the rest of the world. A contributing factor for many years—until the advent of jet travel and instant world communications—was, of course, also the geographic isolation of the United States —between two oceans and with only two countries bordering it—Canada and Mexico.

The primacy of domestic politics in the political thinking of Americans which is having an effect around the world today is thus traditional. In fact, American domestic politics have often had greater influence on the world than American foreign policy. Once again, there is today a widespread mood on the part of Americans in favor of concentrating on solving the problems of America and reducing its world role to a minimum. Do the Americans wish in this way to reach a position from which they can see and deal more effectively? President Johnson said: "Our most reliable guidepost to what we must do in foreign affairs is always what we are doing at home."

George Kennan, a former State Department official and political scientist, warned America, the world power, against this predominance of its domestic affairs: "History will not forgive us our errors because they are explicable on the basis of our domestic politics." The Western world, and especially West Germany, have an interest in keeping the United States from making fatal mistakes in its decisions in international politics. America does not want to play the role of Rome as true ruler of a world realm nor that of a Great Britain as the leading power of an empire. Yet it is, nevertheless, far mightier than either of those imperial powers was when each was at its height.

"The business of America is everybody's business." This sentence is not just an uncomfortable reminder of their responsibilities in world politics for the Americans alone. All of the allies of the United States must see it as a statement of their own potentialities and limitations in international politics.

Neo-isolationist currents are present in contemporary controversies in American domestic politics. An element of historical irony is seen in the fact that neo-isolationist tendencies are currently broadly supported by many liberals. These are the same people who once supported the concept of the United States as the policeman of the democratic world. One must realize, on the basis of statements of politicians and newspaper articles, that a strongly isolationist tendency is a real possibility in the American foreign policy of the near future. But under circumstances similar to those of the domestic controversy in Germany over the new *Ostpolitik*, one is inclined to believe with regard to the American debate on isolationism, that the bark of the new mood is worse than its bite. Much depends on the leadership of America as to the direction the country will take.

A more careful look at the scene of domestic politics in the United States, particularly at Congress, shows that isolationism in a sense of a total retreat from international affairs is out of the question. Even if this idea is fluttering around in the heads of some politicians, there is no way for the United States to practice political isolationism, just as it is impossible for any other nation. The wish for an isolationist existence represents a flight from the realities of world politics in this century into the dream of an age that has passed into oblivion. One can hardly presume such fantasies to exist among the hard-boiled American politicians in the Senate and House of Representatives.

President Nixon is one of those American Presidents who has had to deal with majorities made up by the opposition party in both the House and the Senate. At the moment, the Democrats are in the majority in both houses. And since neo-isolationist arguments in the debate over foreign policy are put forward in that body, there is generally a very real and difficult conflict between the current President and Congress—especially in the case of the Senate. The United States is not standing between isolationism and internationalism; it wants to define its world role in a new way. The discussion deals with how the country's military might should be rationally allocated under the current circumstances of world politics.

As a result of Vietnam, the United States learned the limits of its power. It hopes to avoid similar international debacles from now on, on the basis of more cogent foresight. Thus, the Senate feels it should have a greater part in the relevant decision-making. Its feeling is that there should be no future American involvement without congressional approval. Furthermore, the country's involvement in world politics should also be generally reduced to relieve the need for costly weapons systems and to free more money for domestic needs.

This is only one aspect of the general debate currently going on between the executive and legislative branches of the American government on the division of powers between the two. The debate concerns not only the role of the President vis-à-vis the Congress in the making of all aspects of foreign policy, but also the role of the President vis-à-vis the Congress in the establishment and funding of domestic programs.

All of this involves a review of the American position, but not necessarily a departure from the international political stage.

In the future, American foreign policy will not be decided according to the expression, "Stop the world, I want to get off," but rather by the increasing capacity of the United States to recognize its political limits more clearly and to use its political power more rationally.

3

America's New Role As a World Power

As a superpower, the United States has exercised four main functions: First, the promotion of democratic ideas; second, the provision of nuclear protection for all countries threatened by Communism; third, as the world's leading currency, the dollar has guaranteed economic growth for many countries; and fourth, the United States had stimulated scientific innovation and technological progress as the experimental laboratory for the Western industrial societies. These functions are currently being reexamined.

America was successful in promoting democratic ideas. West Germany and some countries in Western Europe and Asia owe their democratic development during the postwar period to America. After World War II, the United States consciously took over the role of guardian of democracy all over the world. Its self-defined role in international politics was taken for granted and accepted as morally justified by most countries seeking help from the United States. America was welcomed as the police force of the globe, able to guarantee the freedom, security and well-being of other peoples through its military presence and through economic aid.

At that time, the task caught the imagination of America's intellectuals, its business world, and a major part of its organized labor. During the famous fifteen weeks after World War II, the glamorous days of United States foreign policy in the spring of 1947, the policy of containment was conceptualized, and the main strategy of American foreign policy was formulated by the Truman Doctrine and the Marshall Plan. It is no exaggeration to say that for twenty-five years American foreign policy was guided by these theoretical concepts first formulated in that spring of 1947. The policy became the basis for the free development of West Germany. The Americans practiced a policy of constructive cooperation, opposed Communist claims to world hegemony and became a protective power par excellence.

Although successful in Europe and parts of Asia, American foreign policy soon found its limits in the Third World. Here it was much more difficult to decide whether a liberation movement would develop into an anticolonial uprising or a political coup d'état by local Communists guided by remote control from Moscow. Its automatic opposition to such movements made the United States—according to Hans Morgenthau—an antirevolutionary power comparable to Austria under Metternich. After the exodus of the European colonial powers from their foreign possessions and the "independence explosion" which resulted, the United States took over the involvement and the guarantees for many. In effect, it acted everywhere in the world as an antirevolutionary power. It was logical, therefore, that in the Cold War period the Soviet Union should automatically become the guardian of revolution. Furthermore, the United States felt obliged in the course of this process to support regimes whose organization it would ordinarily have had to reject on the basis of its own constitutional principles.

The missionary élan of the United States was critically dampened in the Third World. America was unable to sustain the moral basis of its policy, and it was unable to handle the demands of the Third World in diplomatic terms. The term Ugly American, which originated as the title of a novel written by two Americans, came to be used to describe American involvement in smaller nations as domineering and intrusive. Domestic controversy about Cuba and its political development in a direction opposite to that expected by America as well as American intervention in the Dominican Republic and rumored Central Intelligence Agency roles in Guatemala and elsewhere destroyed the sacred position of American power as the guardian of freedom in the Third World. Even the extraordinary financial support which America gave to developing countries throughout the world could no longer make a dent in this popular impression.

When the schism between China and the Soviet Union finally became definite, America's policy of total anticommunism in the name of freedom became considerably less efficacious. The United States was faced with two centers of communism characterized by different political trends, different methods, and rivalry. At the same time, signs of separate national interests emerging within the Communist bloc provided an opportunity for new efforts at communication—apart from ideological considerations.

At the end of the Cold War, the United States was learning to negotiate with Russia, China, Yugoslavia and other Communist states as well as with dictatorships such as Spain, Greece and Brazil. The democratic missionary zeal of America was being continuously weakened through dimensions of new initiatives and was finally called into question as a whole by Vietnam. Since then America has seen its own socio-political order questioned as a model for freedom in the world, and it has allowed its role as the leading promoter of democratic ideas to be pushed into the background.

The Importance of Aid and Leadership

Today, the international concerns of the United States have been reduced to its basic national interests, and it soberly calculates its risks and gains in foreign policy. Yet during the postwar period when America was able to fulfill its function as the promoter of democratic ideas convincingly, states came into existence which still continue the tradition of Western democracy. If America were about to abandon its role as the leading democratic power, these states could not remain indifferent. West Germany is one of these states. Furthermore, the United States will not be able without a minimum of democratic support to remain the decisive pillar supporting its effectiveness in avoiding conflicts, above all in the Third World.

One can naturally not look at these salutary functions apart from America's functions as a nuclear and economic power, because the American missionary idea faded with the leveling-off of its nuclear and economic might. Since the Soviet Union has drawn even with the United States as a nuclear power, America is no longer a nuclear guardian that can guarantee the freedom of other states in each case. If we remember that today America itself is susceptible to a nuclear strike, the reliability of the American nuclear guarantee is at least questionable. When America's own survival is at stake, its allies cannot expect help at any price.

Since the Soviet Union first faced the United States as an equal nuclear power, a sense of nuclear responsibility has evolved. The notion of nuclear protection of other states has lost its primacy to solving the question of how a nuclear conflict can be avoided in the first place. In this context, the United States and the Soviet Union have shared a high level of responsibility. To their own surprise, this process has made them realize common interests not shared by any other nations in the world. On both sides, this responsibility has led to a reduction in the importance of ideological considerations. Today both want to limit the nuclear arms race and to prevent the proliferation of nuclear weapons.

In the economic field, three formidable rivals of America have appeared: the Common Market, Germany, and Japan. As the leading currency of the world, the dollar was the most visible sign of America's third function as the world's leading economic power. In fact, the defense alliances with the European nations and Japan were initiated by the United States primarily on the basis of economic motives. The economic equilibrium in the world would have been disturbed considerably, if even a few of these states had fallen under Communist control. It is true that the commercial interests behind the policies of the United States have always been exaggerated, particularly from the Marxist point of view, but there can be little doubt that the industrial and commercial capacities of the United States have developed a source of might which has made America a superpower in the economic realm as well.

This process included a comprehensive program of

economic, military and humanitarian aid to most of the states in the world, for which the United States has spent $150 to $200 billion since the end of World War II. When at the end of October, 1971, the United States Senate resolved to cut foreign aid drastically, the consternation aroused around the world was as large as that aroused in America's executive branch. This decision was not final, but it still highlighted the importance of American aid for the world. While American aid has shown only limited success in the developing countries to this day and often has not resulted in a gain of political support, Western Europe and Japan have become great trading nations and economic powers as a result of assistance from the United States.

Although much slandered today and in danger of being dethroned as the leading currency of the world, the dollar played a dominant role in this postwar economic recovery. It was one of the functions of the United States as a postwar superpower to oversee the fate of the Western economies. But domestic economic problems made it increasingly clear to America that it could no longer exercise its function as the economic foundation of the Western world indefinitely, and the chronic deficit in the American balance of payments since the sixties is certainly indicative of the overinvolvement of the United States.

Yet, it is this economic sphere that lends itself most readily to cooperation with, and participation by, other nations such as West Germany, the other Western European states, and Japan. All of these countries can and must shoulder some of the burdens previously carried by the United States alone. One should not forget that it was American foreign aid provided to the industrial states of Western Europe and Japan after World

War II that gave the impetus to the miracle of economic recovery of these countries. Yet, foreign aid continues to be necessary; the developing countries are as much as ever in need of it. Therefore foreign aid must continue, and American interest must be revived through the cooperation of the Western industrial nations. This is all the more evident if we recognize that the conflict between the northern and southern hemispheres and between the have and have-not countries currently involves major threats to world peace. It is an absurdity of contemporary world politics that such a critical disparity exists, particularly when one considers the unlimited industrial resources in the developed part of the world as a potential for helping the underdeveloped countries. One would like to anticipate in the seventies an international constellation in which the United States would be the leading power among the industrial countries cooperating to help the Third World. Such cooperation would also include the states of Western Europe, Australia and Canada. The objective would be to reduce the economic gap throughout the world. Some theoreticians of international politics also see a role for the Soviet Union and its Eastern European satellites as eventual members of the group of developed nations devoted to the alleviation of poverty in the world. America must continue to exercise the economic functions of a superpower, but it must be supported from now on by the industrial nations that have achieved similar status.

There is no doubt that America will remain the leading power among the industrial states. It will be sustained in this role particularly if it continues to exercise its fourth superpower function as a laboratory for industrial development. A characteristic of superpowers is not only that they have more extensive resources at their disposal than other states do, but also that their political weight in international politics is determined by large-scale technological research and development efforts. The future of industrial society in general will be determined largely by the United States. Even if current appreciation of America's role is qualified by some pessimism, the country's continuing record of technological and scientific innovation remains as proof that the United States will continue to maintain its leading role among industrial societies.

In summing up our discussion of the functions of America as a superpower, it seems clear that America has qualified its claim somewhat to be the world power on the side of democracy. On the one hand, its sense of responsibility as the nuclear guardian of the free world has led to a cautious approach regarding military involvement. In the fields of economics, science, and technology, on the other hand, America continues to fully exercise its role as a world power. While the United States is reviewing its superpower status, its foreign policy continues to affect the whole world.

More than forty foreign governments have received commitments on defense and security from the United States. More than seventy states receive American military aid, and over 4,000 treaties and international agreements involve the United States all over the globe. Almost one-and-a-half million American troops are stationed in different parts of the world. These troops are the most visible sign of American presence in foreign countries, along with 375 large military bases and 3,000 of smaller size.

One is tempted to generalize with regard to the results of American world involvement as a superpower. America has been successful where it has been involved with industrial nations. In less developed countries, however, American involvement has been largely unsuccessful. Perhaps it is for this reason that, with the economic recovery of the Western industrial nations, the United States instinctively sees an end to its role as a leading power.

Political discussion in the United States has led to the further conclusion that it is a moot question whether it is *important* for America today to be a leading world power. This discussion in America has taken place during the rise of the Soviet Union to superpower status along with global involvement. In this respect the national images of the two superpowers are plainly antithetical. What the United States has experienced as a pressing burden is for the Soviet Union a valued goal. Many politicians in America have faith in future developments. With typical Anglo-Saxon imperturbability, they think that sooner or later the Soviet Union will also become overinvolved in some part of the world as the United States did in Vietnam. In this context, they point to developments in the Middle East. In any case, America seems to feel on the basis of its own experience that it is questionable whether it should continue to play the role of a leading power.

Columnist Stewart Alsop reported a conversation he had with Winston Churchill in 1948. At that time Churchill sketched the role of the United States as that of a strong horse that wants to pull the rest of the world to peace and affluence. Then, Churchill himself raised the question of whether America would finish this race. To Alsop's surprise, Churchill's answer was no.

Current discussion in America should not lead to a premature conclusion that Churchill's pessimistic view of America's leadership role has already been confirmed.

Economically, militarily, and with respect to industrial and societal innovations, America is still a political power of unprecedented dimensions. It is the geographic and political center of an international system which shows firm political and economic cohesion beyond the merely formal aspect of pacts and aid commitments. The involvement of the United States in world politics is irreversible, not because of the country's treaties, but because of its size and dynamic character. Even in a period in which America concentrates more and more on its domestic tasks and attempts to reform its society, it may attempt to redefine its role in world affairs, but in no way can it eliminate its responsibilities.

The Nixon Doctrine: Let Europe Pay Its Share

President Nixon has described the new scene in world politics. "In the next five to ten years, America must learn to share its leadership position with other centers of power: Western Europe, Japan, the Soviet Union, and China. America does not see the prospects of this constellation as an aggravation but as an alleviation of its world political tasks." Japan and Western Europe are the partners in East and West which are expected to help relieve the United States burden. The dualism in world communism based on Sino-Soviet rivalry will facilitate the negotiations with the Communists. While improved relations with both of the Communist superpowers are already apparent, the prospect of easing the American burden through the contributions of Japan and Western Europe has not been confirmed to any great extent. Japan and Western Europe certainly seem capable of sharing the burden on the basis of their economic strength. But just as the political unification of Western Europe does not seem imminent, Japanese readiness to carry world political responsibility has not yet materialized. President Nixon did speak of a period of five to ten years in which such a development might be possible. But, until then, the United States will have to continue to fulfill its task in world politics as it has in the past. Any reduction in the scope of the task would be to the disadvantage of both developed and underdeveloped states around the world.

The practical policy of the United States, however, seems to be looking toward a reasonable reduction of America's present level of international involvement. It is reexamining its commitments and is searching for ways to reduce them in order to conserve its power. A shift in the motives behind the American involvement in world politics will soon become evident. Features different from those of the early postwar period will emerge. The fear of nuclear war, the hope of gaining large markets in the Communist world, and also the lessons America has learned as a result of its involvement in Asia, all will play a decisive role in its reexamination. With regard to Europe, the readiness of the Europeans themselves for cooperation with the United States will be of great importance.

The conclusions the United States will ultimately draw in its reexamination of its commitments will depend to a great extent on the politics of its allies. The time seems to have come for Western Europeans to stop being on the lookout for changes in American policies in order to adjust to them as quickly as possible. They must now actively participate in the discussion of the

American leadership role. The position of West Germany in the near future will depend critically on the results of such dialogue. Franz Josef Strauss, the leader of the CSU (the Bavarian Christian Social Union, allied with the CDU, Christian Democratic Union) has said, "America can be expected to ask its European allies rather urgently to leave the rows of the peanut gallery, and to accept once again a responsible role onstage."

In the United States, the Nixon administration has brought the discussion of America's leading role in the world into sharp focus. In his inauguration speech on January 20, 1969, Nixon said: "After a period of confrontation we now enter an era of negotiation. It will be known to all people, that during the term of this administration, the channels of communication will be kept open." Nixon has kept his promise. (He was the first American President to visit Moscow and Peking. Roosevelt, who had perhaps cultivated the closest relations with the Soviet Union of any President before Nixon, only traveled as far as Yalta. Other American Presidents, such as Eisenhower and Johnson, had to cancel their Moscow visits because of deteriorating developments in world politics.) The intensive dialogue with the Soviet Union, especially in the SALT (Strategic Arms Limitation) talks, is a focal point of President Nixon's foreign policy aiming at an alleviation of the American burden by negotiating directly with the power involved.

Undoubtedly, the most original contribution of Nixon's foreign policy was his initiative to come to terms with Peking. This political coup which could very easily become a decisive turning point of our time is at the same time essentially a flanking maneuver in negotiations with Moscow.

During the Nixon era of negotiations, some classical principles of diplomacy have been revived in the American efforts to come to terms with the Soviet Union's opponent, China. President Nixon's endeavors to make the United States the active party in the political triangle of America, China, and the Soviet Union are still in an early stage. The result is still to be seen, but there is a method behind the policy: a strategy for international politics known as the Nixon Doctrine.

In the context of the review of American foreign policy that emerged from the entanglement in Asian politics, the essentials of the Nixon Doctrine were quite appropriately announced on the Pacific island of Guam. Through subsequent reports to the Congress, Nixon has developed the doctrine into a fully elaborated concept.

Annual reports on foreign policy delivered by the American President to the Congress are an innovation of the Nixon administration. They represent a comprehensive articulation of official American foreign policy. The first two reports given by President Nixon clearly reveal the influence of Henry Kissinger, his foreign policy adviser. Many ideas which have appeared in the writings of Kissinger since the middle sixties when he was with Harvard's Center for International Affairs have now been incorporated into official American policy. Together with the reports of the Secretary of State, based on more specific aspects of American foreign relations, the Presidential reports provide an important review of official political thinking in America today.

The Nixon Doctrine is the most important element in all such reports. The Doctrine shows a realization of the limits of America's role as a superpower. It proceeds from the notion that America can no longer deal with its overinvolvement in world politics and its crises at home simultaneously. While the Doctrine provides the basis for America's own discussions about its future role in world affairs, it also sets forth guiding principles that America's allies and opponents in world politics should be taking a close look at. To be sure, the Nixon Doctrine still does not provide a complete timetable for American foreign policy goals, from which one can deduce exactly what America will do in the next few years. But it does disclose an intensive search for new political approaches. Clearly, the discussion within the United States on this question is far from over.

In certain instances, the Nixon Doctrine is very precise in its expression of demands and negotiation goals. In other instances, it points only to guidelines for future policy. The Doctrine is consistent with the tradition of American foreign policy in that it is rich with moral insights and aspirations. Yet it would be a mistake to characterize this document as a simple exercise in propaganda. If one reduces the Nixon Doctrine to its basic components, one can see that with this policy statement the United States is in the process of finding a political course for the changing conditions of world politics in the seventies.

There are four basic elements to the Nixon Doctrine: first, a basic affirmation of the responsibility of the United States in international politics; second, an awareness of changes in the alliance commitments of the United States in light of changes in the current international system; third, an attempt to perceive the consequences of the changes in the international strategic balance; and fourth, a view of the polycentrism of the Communist world as a propitious signal for experimentation with new international initiatives.

Clearly all four elements are already manifest in the

foreign policy of the Nixon administration. Nixon has met the domestic proponents of isolationism and the doubters of America's wish to be a world power with explicit acceptance of the country's leading role in international politics. Confronting the isolationists, Nixon has emphasized that it is only a myth of American politics that the country stumbled into its involvement in world affairs. "We are not involved in world affairs because we have commitments. We have commitments because we are involved." Nixon has emphasized that the alliance commitments of the country are derived from the interests of America itself. In the future as well, the commitments must remain oriented towards the interests of the United States.

These are more sober words than those of the missionary statements of Truman and Eisenhower. What is clearly stated is that the United States has concluded its alliances on the basis of its own interests and not just out of altruism. For the same reasons, Nixon has clearly accepted the continuing international commitment of the United States. He wants to establish these American commitments on a lasting basis. To this end he supports local and regional alliance initiatives as well as national independence to forge a stronger peace. In fact, these thoughts are evidenced in many of the speeches of the American President. He leaves no doubt that steadfastness of the country's acceptance of its alliance commitments also involves critical scrutiny of those alliances. But he knows that while the United States must redefine its world role, vestiges of past arrangements will persist. Thus, one cannot speak of an end to the era of United States leadership in the world, but rather the beginning of a new role.

Nixon recognizes that many nations wonder about

the competence of the Americans for world leadership. He does not feel that a general retreat of America from world involvement for the purpose of contemplating its role is desirable. But he does feel that contemporary international conditions are appropriate to demonstrate the leadership competence of the United States. This attitude is particularly clear in his feeling toward America's allies. But Nixon's America is no longer willing to carry the responsibility alone. It wants the active support of its partners in accordance with their potential. In a way, this question involves the application to international politics of the subsidy concept of the social teachings of the Roman Catholic Church. Help will be accorded only to the man who is ready to help himself. The view from Washington is: The concern of Americans for defense should not be greater than that of their allies, nor should the efforts of the Americans be more extensive than those of the people whom they are supporting.

This new American alliance strategy was first put into practice in the Vietnamization process. The United States will not take the affairs and problems of its allies any more seriously than they do themselves. In the context of West Germany, this means that the Americans will not be more German than the Germans.

Nixon is defining new forms of partnership between the United States and its allies, and he has stated what these are in practical terms. "The new partnership finds its physical expression in larger material contributions by the other nations." This sentence out of the Nixon Doctrine might just as well have been written in German and Japanese, rather than English, since it is directed particularly at those two booming commercial nations. The new partnership Nixon is after not only expects a broader share of the costs of the political program to be accepted by its allies, but the allies are also expected to take on a larger role in the formulation of alliance policy.

The allies of the United States should know that America is ending its role as a soloist in international politics. It wants to loosen its allies from their static positions and encourage them to more active political participation on their own. From now on the United States will be unwilling to carry the responsibility for complicated decisions on its own shoulders alone. How the training of an army should be organized, what will be necessary to the conceptualization and implementation of a given set of development plans, what form of economic policy a state chooses, and how a regional alliance should take shape—all of these are questions to which the United States will want to hear the responses of its allies from now on before it gets involved itself. The allies in question should not wonder to what extent the details of the Nixon Doctrine touch each of them individually. Such a question is already too reminiscent of the past in which the United States generally delivered prescriptions for the political behavior of its allies. The future policy of the allies should not be to ask questions and wait for the answers from the United States but to approach the Americans with suggestions and to participate actively in joint considerations. In Nixon's words, "If we were today to attempt to determine the character of the new diplomacy completely on our own, we would fall back into the arrogant forms of behavior of the past, and just in this way contradict the spirit of our new attitude."

The partners of the United States must now get used to the idea that alliances with America are no longer only the business of the Americans. This suggests a solution to an old problem in American diplomatic relations with its allies. The late Secretary of State, Dean Acheson, once described the problem in an anecdote. After a European-American conference, the American delegate walked towards the door of the conference hall with the French and German delegates. He was wondering how to avoid having the Frenchman and the German try to decide who should go through the door first. If he were just to go straight through himself, the American reflected, the Europeans would think: typical American, always pushing ahead. So he decided to go through the door arm-in-arm with both delegates at once. This plan was successful, though not without a little crowding. Only a moment after the American had left the two foreigners, the Frenchman commented: typical American, no culture.

Americans foresee a process of healthy development in the intellectual climate fostered by the new relationship. The United States as well as its allies will be obliged to consider some political problems that had perhaps earlier been removed from the daily agenda of all nations or perhaps never even made it onto the agenda in the first place. In this sense, Nixon sees the beginning of the end of the postwar period. International politics is no longer in the hands of the United States alone. America's allies must be ready to participate as well.

The foundations of the alliance shall continue to be guaranteed by the United States. Nixon sees these in three areas: "First, the United States will respect all of its alliance commitments. Second, we shall provide a protective shield in the event a nuclear power threatens the freedom of an ally or a nation whose existence we consider vital to our security. Third, in instances in which other forms of aggression are involved, we shall provide military and economic aid if it is required from us in accordance with our alliance commitments."

As clearly as the Nixon Doctrine delineates the new forms of the partnership, the conclusions that it reaches on the basis of the new world strategic balance are unclear. For example, one assumes that the United States is saying that it cannot remain the responsibility of the United States alone to provide a first line of defense. This is more or less the basic concept on which the demand to other nations for increased responsibility for their own self-defense is based. Thus, every threatened nation is to carry on the main responsibility for the establishment of the military forces necessary for its own defense. This basic concept is related to America's announcement of a major reconsideration of its military commitments. Even binding agreements should be seen in terms of a dynamic process. Clearly hinted at in this context are troop deployments whose purpose and necessity must be adjusted to changing conditions. The United States still sees its overseas presence and its direct military involvement in foreign countries as an important task. Yet Nixon has warned against neglect of modern realities of defense questions in the regular cutbacks in defense appropriations. He has indicated that the vote against defense appropriations should not ossify into a kind of ritual.

The questions raised as to whether the United States can still afford a nuclear commitment to other nations leads to a conclusion that is very unpopular in America today. If America is not in a position to use its nuclear weapons to support other threatened countries, all nations that can produce their own nuclear weapons will do so. But, from the point of view of the Nixon Doctrine, this would be a destabilizing development. Above all, the mere mathematical probability that conflicts could lead to nuclear world catastrophe would grow. The commitments of the United States in this area are defined out of a sober sense of nuclear responsibility, for it knows that where it does not take a stand, a new potential for nuclear armament might result. For this reason, the United States feels that it must continue to provide a nuclear guarantee. Here, an explicit language of nuclear responsibility stands in the stead of enthusiastic alliance commitments. Once again, in this context, Japan and West Germany are the countries to which the American concern is most strongly directed.

The fourth element of the Nixon Doctrine involves a tactical maneuver of American foreign policy. In its policy directed towards the Communist world, it aims at taking advantage of polycentrism, the major result of the schism between China and the Soviet Union.

The United States is interested in bilateral agreements with any of the Eastern European satellites of the Soviet Union that show independent interests. Nixon's visits to Eastern Europe have emphasized the opportunities that the United States sees for political developments here.

From the point of view of West Germany, all of the elements of the Nixon Doctrine combine to provide a stimulus for an innovative policy with the United States. Action along these lines must not result from a fear of rapid American disengagement from Europe. But Germany's policy should attempt to hinder any developments which might lead to American overestimation of West Germany's capability of defending itself and an

American conclusion that German security needs are no longer in accord with reality.

The Nixon Doctrine is not an end to discussion of the future policies of the United States. It does, however, show how strongly the official foreign policy of America already reflects current public opinion in the country. The isolationist trends are unmistakable. Today, the successes of American Presidents are seen in terms of the termination of alliances rather than their development or initiation.

4

Americans and Russians at the Negotiating Table

When the Americans and the Russians sit down alone at the negotiating table, they are accompanied by the hopes and the suspicions of the rest of the world. The other nations "hope" because they want to see the tensions between the superpowers eased. Yet, they are also "suspicious" because they fear that the superpowers may make agreements at the expense of the rest of the world.

In a comparison of the 1970 defense budgets of the United States and the Soviet Union, the Institute for Strategic Studies in London estimated the following figures: $79.2 billion for the United States, $48.8 billion for the Soviet Union. If the rapidly increasing defense costs are to be kept in some reasonable proportion to general economic growth, both states will have to cut back on their rates of expenditure or at least freeze them at the present levels. Yet, everyone knows that these budget figures are in no way the actual figures for the full defense sectors. In fact, expenditures run at a much higher level. For example, expenditures for research and development often do not show up as direct costs in military budgets, but instead are scattered throughout a government's total budget. The United States has finally begun to feel the domestic consequences of its international involvement and high defense costs. In the Soviet Union as well, argument as to whether heavy industry or the consumer goods sector is to be emphasized concerns the entire Soviet leadership. But to get down to negotiations on the basis of these parallel economic concerns, both the Americans and the Russians have to forget a number of historical differences and ideological prejudices. It remains unclear on the diplomatic scene whether the Russians are in a position to let ideology as a factor fade into the background. Certainly, in the context of their rivalry with the other Communist world power, China, they have not been able to ignore the ideological component of their foreign policy.

The Americans also face problems concerning ideology. Their Western European allies expect American loyalty to democratic principles when it comes to negotiations with the Russians even though these European allies have criticized many ideological aspects of American policy in the Western Hemisphere or in Asia. Even if the United States has currently made it clear that it is not interested in Soviet domestic affairs and even though the Soviet Union now speaks only tongue-in-cheek of world revolution, both powers still find it difficult to ignore completely the ideologies that each stands for. The situation is only that much more difficult since the history of the relations between the two countries during the postwar period has involved a series of confrontations and crises with ideological overtones.

One can say that every part of the world has been touched in some way by stresses and strains in the relations between the two powers. The crises in Berlin, the Middle East, Cuba, and finally the wars in Korea and

Vietnam, have been crises to which the term "Cold War" could only be applied as an extraordinarily mild euphemism.

Today, the United States must try to normalize relations with its onetime comrade-in-arms despite the barrier of hostile feelings that has built up during the postwar period. According to President Nixon, America and the Soviet Union owe it to their own peoples as well as the peoples of the world to undertake an attempt at negotiation. One thing is immediately very clear in this context. Neither world power is interested in some all-encompassing arrangement. For this, both lack not only the will but also the ability. Instead, the United States and the Soviet Union have sorted out a number of specific matters they both believe are particularly susceptible to negotiation. First of all, there is the question of how to avoid direct nuclear collision. Second, the two superpowers want to hold their financial burdens for armaments within tolerable limits. Third, both countries want to defend their current nuclear monopolies against a proliferation of atomic capabilities among nonnuclear nations.

Without doubt, the longest and most significant negotiations have come from the attempts of both superpowers to achieve a limitation of strategic weapons (the SALT talks). Conferences have been held in Helsinki and Vienna since 1969. And if the international scene is to be spared a return to primitive Cold War conditions, these negotiations will undoubtedly continue for some time. The political payoff of these talks lies in the potential end to the nuclear arms race between the superpowers. This undertaking is certainly the most exciting aspect of current détente politics.

SALT I led to two agreements, and President

Nixon traveled to Moscow to sign the two documents with Leonid Brezhnev on May 26, 1972. The first agreement was a treaty of limitation of antiballistic missile (ABM) systems. Both treaty partners limited themselves to two ABM systems of 100 missiles each in separate locations. One system was to be deployed for the defense of the national capital and the other for the defense of certain land-based launching pads for intercontinental ballistic missiles (ICBM). The second agreement was an interim agreement on specific means for the limitation of strategic offensive weapons. It was agreed upon for a period of five years and essentially froze the number of launching facilities for ICBM's and submarine-launched ballistic missiles (SLBM) on both sides at the existing level in 1972.

Problems related to the first agreement were evidenced by a series of added interpretive notes which contained important additional provisions. There were also several unilateral statements appended to the agreement, among which, one made by the United States deserves special attention. The United States reserved the right to withdraw from the conditions of the ABM treaty if a further treaty on the general limitation of strategic offensive weapons were not concluded within the five years of the interim agreement. For its part, the Soviet Union states that it aimed at the inclusion of all SLBM's controlled by America's NATO allies in the final limitation treaty. The Americans had rejected this point.

Thus, we arrive at the basic problems of SALT II. In the ensuing discussion of offensive weapons, the Soviet Union will attempt once again to include the nuclear weapons controlled by NATO forces. *Ostpolitik* in this context is proceeding at a very high level of suspense.

Political negotiations on the subject of Berlin led to an easing of tensions over what could have been a critical point of conflict between the two superpowers. Without doubt, the Berlin Agreement of 1971 that resulted from one and one-half years of talks relaxed the negotiating climate between the United States and the Soviet Union. The very close tie between the German *Ostpolitik* and the *Ostpolitik* pursued by the United States becomes especially visible in the successful American effort leading to the Four Power Agreement on Berlin. The Berlin Agreement offered hope for the first time that the security of West Berlin was greater than it had ever been since 1949.

Nixon's eight-day visit to Moscow was assuredly an indication of the relaxed political relations in the international triangle currently taking shape. It was not really so much a question of the results of the visit in the form of signed agreements on tariffs, scientific and technical matters, as well as the SALT agreements. Far more important was the atmosphere of the visit which made it clear that basic changes were in the works in the relations between the United States and the Soviet Union. The visit took place even though the United States had just initiated a particularly hard line towards Moscow's ally, North Vietnam, by the mining of the harbors of that country. Confrontation in one location clearly did not keep the superpowers from demonstrating their cooperation in another—a new, cool realism which would have been unthinkable during the Cold War.

In the same context, it was almost a sensation for the inner structure of the Communist countries that President Nixon could make a television address to the citizens of the Soviet Union. Finally, at the end of Nixon's visit, the United States and the Soviet Union confirmed in a joint twelve-point statement their will to cooperate with each other.

Since Nixon's visit, the Americans have officially conceded parity of the Soviet nuclear force vis-à-vis the United States. It is symptomatic of the changes in the contemporary international system that this military advance on the part of the Soviets occurred at the same time that the readiness for cooperation on many levels was declared by both superpowers.

In fact, cooperation had already been under way before Nixon's arrival in the Russian capital. This was apparent in the agreements waiting in Moscow for the President to sign. An agreement was reached forbidding the stationing of nuclear weapons and other means of mass destruction on the ocean floor, a considerable success in the efforts directed towards disarmament. Both superpowers are working in this area together with twenty-five other nations in Geneva under a mandate from the United Nations General Assembly. The more than five hundred sessions held during the past ten years have not been in vain. A number of noteworthy results have been achieved. The nuclear test ban treaty, the nonproliferation treaty, and the treaty banning nuclear weapons in outer space have been some results that one might not have dared to hope for on the basis of the past history of disarmament conferences.

Other questions, related to the ocean floor and international law of the sea, have been taken up in negotiations. Negotiations were initiated aimed at the prevention of naval incidents. In March 1970, the signing of the nonproliferation treaty signaled another successful conclusion to American-Soviet efforts. Diplomatic contacts between the two superpowers were broadened when consulates were opened in San Francisco and Leningrad.

One of the twelve points in the basic statement of aims issued in Moscow involved the improvement of commercial ties between the United States and the Soviet Union. In a message to Congress in 1971, Nixon had said: "We are both great industrial powers but nevertheless have very little commercial contact with each other. We would both profit substantially if our ties were to allow an increase in trade." But the leaders of the Soviet Union have a problem concerning their image of Communism. In view of the economic growth that one might expect as well as the changes concomitant with industrial development, there is a danger that the Soviet system which they have wanted to portray to the world as appealing might turn out to be a failure. (It is no secret, of course, that Soviet agricultural policy has consistently failed to meet Soviet goals.)

The United States itself has been forced to concern itself specifically with ways of mastering the changes involved in the transition from an industrial to a postindustrial society. In a similar context, the Russians will have to devote a great deal of energy to domestic challenges if they wish to avoid disavowing Communism totally as a model for social life. The enormous defense budgets that both maintain show what large economic problems must be resolved. In fact, the Soviet Union has been falling increasingly behind the United States as an economic power and is running the risk of falling behind Japan and the Common Market countries as well.

Finally, it still remains to be shown whether the crisis in the Soviet bloc, which found its apex in Soviet intervention in Czechoslovakia, has come to an end or is still smoldering. The Polish riots at the end of 1970 offered evidence supporting the latter condition. To relieve some of the problems involved in establishing commercial relations, a communiqué was signed in Moscow establishing a joint American-Soviet trade mission, but the repeated visits of officials from the U.S. Department of Commerce to Moscow have shown that many obstacles to trade still have to be overcome.

Even so, a number of noteworthy American investment projects in the Soviet Union have already been discussed, and some agreements have already been signed. The economy of the United States is urgently searching for new markets and wants to make full use of its productive capacities. President Nixon has made a firm decision to provide strong support for the development of this East-West trade. But the Russians themselves want—and need—more Western technical and scientific know-how to be able to deal more effectively with the future. The Americans and the Russians declared their commitment to cooperation in the twelve-point statement of aims. In this context as well, cooperative efforts in space will provide a dramatic symbol for this détente. All of these activities show that in the future, Americans and Russians would seem to prefer to sit at a table with each other as businessmen, scientists, and technicians rather than as diplomats and soldiers.

Nixon wants to negotiate with the Soviet leaders, and for the present and the foreseeable future, relations between the two superpowers are to be straightened out at the negotiating table. There is broad support for this policy in the United States, even though rejection of Communism and anti-Soviet feeling are deeply rooted in the United States. Usually, the Soviet Union receives unfavorable press coverage in America today only as a result of specific incidents. This was particularly the case when a Lithuanian fled from a Soviet ship onto a U.S. Coast Guard boat. He was retrieved by the Russians as the Americans watched without intervening. So used to freedom of movement themselves, the Americans were provided through this incident with a renewed and clear example of the dictatorial character of the Soviet regime. It raised high waves of controversy in the United States and led to strict instructions to American officials to actively support such refugee attempts. Another situation, which has prompted anti-Soviet demonstrations by many Jewish groups in the United States, concerns the requirements of the Soviet Union for exit visas for Russian Jews.

There have been occasional disturbances in the American-Soviet negotiating climate in the context of world politics as well. First of all, there has been the attempt by the Soviet Union to establish itself as a nuclear power in the Caribbean. In spite of the setback suffered in the Cuban missile crisis of 1962, the Russians have never given up their interest in this objective. It is, in fact, nothing but a Soviet copy of Dulles's policy of encirclement—a plan essentially identified with the Cold War. Like the Western Hemisphere, the Asian theater has continually supplied explosive situations which could lead to a reversal in the current trend of friendly negotiations to active confrontation. The Russians see Nixon's China policy as a move against them, even though on the occasion of his visit to Canada in October of 1971, Soviet Prime Minister Kosygin stated that the President's contact with Peking was a good thing.

On the other hand, Russian involvement in India makes it clear that the Soviet Union can make countermoves with an active Asian policy of its own. The Soviet-Indian Friendship Treaty can be understood as a direct Russian answer to the attempts of the Americans and Chinese to establish relations with each other. In the long-term conflict between India and Pakistan, the Soviet Union has sided with India while China has supported Pakistan. Thus, the Soviet-Indian Friendship Treaty offered political support for the Indian invasion of East Pakistan. In term of international politics, however, the Soviet Union, by concluding the treaty with India, was actually taking aim at China and the United States. In this manner, it made its own interests in Asia clear to the two other world powers. The Americans were quite startled by this Soviet-Indian agreement, but for too long the United States had neglected the Indians. During this period, in any case, Indian neutrality had slowly been giving way to a pro-Soviet orientation as the Indians came closer and closer to an outbreak of hostilities with the Pakistanis.

While the United States is still involved in its attempts to reach an understanding with China, the Soviet Union has scored a major coup. It was successful in incorporating the almost five hundred million Indians into its alliance system. These developments in Asia show that the current round of negotiations between the two superpowers does not necessarily guarantee the security of their spheres of influence. The Kremlin sees itself threatened in Eastern Europe by the new China policy of the United States to the extent that states like Romania and Yugoslavia might conceivably follow the example of Albania and lean increasingly towards China. The Soviets have long feared such a development and the potential it might provide to countries within the Eastern European bloc to gain more leeway for action against the Soviet Union. Again in this context, the Russians see realization of their interests being curtailed by the Americans. All of these developments show that an era of confrontation could still rapidly reappear out of the current era of negotiation.

Averell Harriman, former American Ambassador in Moscow and witness to countless important negotiations between the superpowers, is cautious in his estimation of the prospects for future Soviet-American relations. He has said: "On the one hand, I am not a prophet; on the other hand, it is particularly dangerous to speak prophetically about the political development of the Soviet Union." As a consequence, Nixon is prepared for two alternatives: a Soviet Union that is ready for peaceful arrangements or one that reverts to the methods of confrontation.

The condition of the world today does not point to the actuality of one of these two alternatives more than that of the other, but rather to a combination of both. The world should probably get used to an image of a Russian bear that is both smiling and frowning at the same time. Nixon seems to be the only American President other than Kennedy to have recognized this fact in the postwar period. He was Vice President himself when he discussed the future with the then Soviet chief, Khrushchev, at a Moscow exhibition. Khrushchev prophesied a life under Communism for the grandchildren of Nixon's generation. Nixon rejected the prospect with sharp words.

That so-called "kitchen debate" became known around the world. It characterized the old role of the superpowers as the leaders of two distinct political blocs. Even in the current negotiations, neither party can escape these old roles completely. Yet perhaps a new bilateral relationship will develop from a give-and-take process that could result in new contours for the international politics of the seventies. In case of emergency, at any rate, communication between the two giants has been improved. Since September 1971, a "hot line" between the two countries has existed to prevent accidental outbreak of nuclear war as a result of misunderstanding.

5

The New Partnership with Europe

Even at a time when the Americans are aiming at an easing of their international burdens, the approach of the United States to its alliance commitments still receives extremely favorable press coverage in Europe. At the same time, the social and political problems of the United States and the new isolationist currents in that country have aroused anxiety among Europeans with regard to America's intentions. And the Europeans themselves have not yet agreed to take on the new role that the United States has allotted them in the alliance.

From America's point of view, Europe has grown out of the role of protégé to become an equal partner with whom these burdens can be shared. Nixon calls this the "mature partnership." Americans are asking openly why two hundred million Americans should still be protecting three hundred million Europeans who are living in healthy social and economic conditions. As Henry Kissinger has put it, the founding years of Atlantic politics are now past.

This situation is apparent in the behavior of European politicians as well. It is no longer self-evident in the 1970s that one should simply accept American suggestions and be satisfied as much as possible with only a limited influence on American policies in view of Washington's international preeminence. After having contended with each other to gain access to Washington, European politicians are now racing to Moscow. Whereas trips of European politicians to the United States used to be a source of political glamour, today it would seem that it is a visit to Moscow that provides the headlines that these politicians need for their domestic support. European *Ostpolitik* is of more immediate importance to them at the moment than American world politics.

The United States knows that Europe is still not ready today to be a full partner in international political undertakings. Henry Kissinger has put it this way: "Europeans do not feel that their interests are at stake where the United States is involved outside of Europe." Americans have learned this lesson from the war in Vietnam. They know today that their involvement in Asia worries the Europeans and is not appreciated by them. They could not convince the Europeans to join them in pursuit of the common goals of the Western world in Asia. The Europeans, however, have behaved in a somewhat contradictory manner. While they question whether all means of warfare can be justified in the effort to contain Communism in Asia, they expect an unlimited American nuclear guarantee for Europe.

In any case, it is arguable as to just what conclusions are to be drawn from the analysis of current international politics and how burdens should be divided between Europe and the United States. The questions are not being raised by Europeans. The Americans are the ones who are asking them. In the past, there was no talk in the United States about the sharing of burdens. But the heart of the portions of the Nixon Doctrine that are relevant to Europe lies in the policy that Europe must not only cooperate but actually carry its own part of the responsibilities for the defense of the West. The European countries have already stated their intention to strengthen their conventional forces in the NATO communiqué of December 1970. But the concept of deterrence carried over by the Nixon Doctrine into the realm of defense calls once again for strengthened conventional forces among the European countries.

The political goals of the Atlantic partnership have also been redefined. As early as October 1966, Lyndon Johnson set forth the new elements of the European policies of the United States at a national conference of American newspaper editors. Johnson went beyond the standard themes that called for a modernization of NATO and improvement of Atlantic institutions to name the integration of the Western European community and new efforts at East-West relations as goals of American foreign policy for Europe. Americans look to a united Europe for decisive relief of their political and military burdens. This process is to be further supported through an easing of the tensions with the East. Since that time, diplomatic chores in the Atlantic Alliance have increased. Improvement of East-West relations is now actively pursued parallel to the problems of security and European stability.

Johnson's policy for Europe was to be built on three pillars: a new élan for the Atlantic Alliance; movement towards Western European unity; and improvement of East-West relations. Johnson emphasized his support for the third element of this policy with a long list of political and economic efforts directed towards the East. The initiative had its impact on European thinking. It is open to question whether the Atlantic Alliance has gained any new élan or whether real progress has been made towards European unity. But the nations of Europe actively took up the call for *Ostpolitik*.

An active *Ostpolitik* has become the sign of the autonomy of the European states from America, but the Americans have watched its development with confidence and composure. They know only too well that there could hardly be an arrangement between Europe and the Soviet Union that wouldn't involve a more immediate risk for the Europeans than for themselves. Some years ago, former Secretary of State Dean Rusk said: "We have no quarrel with the Communists. We are involved in this conflict on behalf of the interests of other people." The Europeans have acted with independence towards the East. In the context of their defense, however, they continue in full dependence on the nuclear guarantee of the United States.

The basic question concerning European-American relations is whether the Europeans can remain confident of the American promise of nuclear defense. It is true that no one today in the United States or Europe seriously believes in a direct military threat from the Soviet Union. The peoples of Western Europe are essentially free from any fear of war. But they are, nevertheless, faced with the fact that the military might of the Warsaw Pact forces has grown in the past few years, and that there has been no sign of any end to this growth. Since the end of World War II, Western Europe has experienced enough crises and attempts at aggression initiated by the Soviet Union. If Europeans today feel secure from the threat of attack from the East, this is not a result of Russia's expressed love of peace, but of the strength of the Atlantic Alliance. The foundation of the

Atlantic Alliance is the nuclear protection offered by the United States. If Europe wants to continue to be able to pursue its *Ostpolitik* from secure ground, the nuclear guarantee of the United States must remain beyond doubt.

The United States and Europe face the necessity of developing a joint political agenda once again, if they are going to negotiate with the East. They must work out a common position on the military problems of troop reductions, disarmament efforts, and the European Security Conference.

Beyond this, the Europeans will have to follow developments on the American scene with increased attention. They must recognize the challenges they face in the changes in the alliance with the United States and the greater efforts demanded from them. As Western industrial nations with liberal political systems, the European countries will continue to have a useful basis for cooperation with the United States. But as the creation of a partner of equal weight to America, the political fusion of Western Europe is a critical prerequisite to an Atlantic Alliance of balanced partners. A politically unified Europe could no longer limit itself to its conventional role in the context of sharing the burdens of the joint defense. In cooperation with the United States, it would have to be in a position to make a credible contribution on its own to a nuclear deterrence strategy. Only such a development would permit the sought-after balance in the Atlantic partnership and allow the United States greater freedom once again in its international political activities.

Certainly these developments require new thinking on the part of the United States. America can no longer look at the division of burdens within the alliance from the point of view of a leading power that expects European military efforts without sufficient nuclear security. But only the political unification of Europe and the will to work together in the nuclear dimension as well can stimulate such a change in the American point of view.

Now that Great Britain has entered the Common Market, it is up to European politicians to decide whether they will begin to play European power politics in the style of the nineteenth century once again or whether they are ready to pull the whole political power of Europe into the Western alliance. The latter prospect promises not only increased security but also a better basis for negotiations with the East.

Nixon has called 1973 the "year of Europe." It is no accident that he did this at a time when American involvement in Indochina was nearing its end. "The year of Europe: What will it be like?" an American commentator has asked. "When I was in Korea, it was the year of the tiger. But I never saw a tiger." But European-American problems cannot wait any longer. The urgent questions regarding trade and currency matters have shown this repeatedly. And the political negotiations behind the current MBFR (Multilateral and Balanced Force Reduction) talks and the European Security Conference (KSZE in German) also call for Atlantic consultation. It would not be difficult for the "year of Europe" to lead to a few years of intensive European-American negotiations that could bring about conditions for a new partnership.

Japan—The Shocked Ally

Interest in Japan's role in world politics has grown with the new developments in United States-China relations. This development is readily explained by the traditional rivalry between China and Japan, which has been emphasized again and again by Chou En-lai. China-watchers even claim that China's main motive for coming to new terms with the United States is its fear of Japan. The disengagement of the Americans from Asia, based on the Nixon doctrine, further disquiets the Chinese. In Nixon's exhortation to America's political partners in Asia to help themselves, they see an invitation to Japan to become militarily active once again.

As a result of American policy under the Nixon doctrine, questions have been raised within Japan regarding its future relationship with the United States. The same is true within West Germany. In fact, the relationships of both Japan and West Germany with the United States seem to have developed along parallel lines over the years. There are solid historical reasons why this is so.

Both countries were the wartime enemies of the United States and were defeated. Both, with the help of America, were able to make a quick economic recovery and achieve status as leading economic world powers within a short period of time. Both countries today are major rivals of the United States in international trade and, despite the close relationship of both countries to the United States, both have also felt themselves hard hit by the international economic policies of the United States. Both have believed that they have been the target of unfair American official and unofficial criticism and policies concerning international trade and investment matters. (In this context, the Japanese have spoken of a second national defeat.) And both, because of their special relationship with the United States, have been forced consistently to make concessions on currency questions.

While the United States has used an iron hand in dealing with its two allies in the international economic sphere, its action—or lack of action—or hesitancy—in the political area has caused doubts in both Japan and West Germany concerning American reliability. For example, the Americans seem somewhat uncertain themselves, in light of the contemporary conditions of international politics, concerning the extent to which they can continue to stand solidly with their partners in their commitment of unconditional guarantee of nuclear protection. What will be the effect of new American foreign policy moves on this guarantee? While in Europe United States disengagement has only been discussed, in Asia an extensive withdrawal of the American presence is already underway. This action, along with the enunciation by the United States of its new China policy, has given a sense of insecurity to Japan. For, faced with a China that is a nuclear power, the basic question for Japan—as it is for West Germany, albeit in a different environment—is: Can the nuclear guarantee of the Americans be relied upon? Both countries have signed the nuclear nonproliferation treaty. Were Japan to conclude on the basis of new political developments in China that as a modern power it should have atomic weapons at its disposal, presumably West Germany would also want to examine this option even though it would have to consider such a development in a European rather than a national context.

Another example concerns the drastic change in United States policy towards China. As a result, the Japanese have had to look for new initiatives in their own relations with that country, and the new China policy in Japan has developed as a kind of parallel to West Germany's new *Ostpolitik*. Fortunately, for both countries, their strong ties to America seem to be able to survive such sharp shifts. For Germany, the improving American-Soviet dialogue provided an incentive to begin negotiations with Moscow directly. Similarly, Nixon's visit to Peking was followed by a Japanese visit to China's capital.

One question, however, is whether the sense of insecurity concerning the United States as a reliable alliance partner will result in widespread criticism. There have been many strong anti-American currents and demonstrations in Japan. In Germany, anti-Americanism seemed for a long time to be confined to student protests, but now has partially spilled over to public opinion as well.

Despite all of these moves and concerns, however, according to official statements in Japan and Germany, the alliance is still alive. The words of former Japanese Prime Minister Sato might have been spoken by Willy Brandt: "It is very hard to imagine that the United States might withdraw. We are very happy about the apparent end of the war in Vietnam. But peace in Asia depends on American policy in Asia. It is certainly not necessary to maintain expensive armed forces at the present level of strength, but a U.S. presence is necessary. We are confident in Nixon's assurance that the United States will do nothing new that might disappoint old friends." In this official statement that American policy in Asia remains basically the same, the door is opened nevertheless for future efforts to find a new model for the alliance.

If the United States actually wants to remain as the leading power among the Western industrial nations in the future, the realization of this aspiration will depend largely on America's capability to continue to develop a set of alliance relationships satisfactory to the security interests of both Japan and West Germany. The Nixon Doctrine, in claiming to be more than a synonym for isolationism, can only be successful if the United States does not limit its energies to new negotiations with China and the Soviet Union, but also dedicates itself intensively to the cultivation of its ties with Japan and West Germany. For their part, Japan and Germany must see the Nixon Doctrine as an opportunity to work with the United States in a new structuring of their own relationships. Both perhaps have for too long been concerned with their own special political problems—West Germany with the reunification question and the Japanese with the Okinawa question. Perhaps both have spent too much time on these single issues to the detriment of other political issues that have confronted them.

In principle, West Germany and Japan should make an effort to overcome a basic policy that has developed from their long-standing position under American protection; that is, the exercise of international economic power without political responsibility. They are no longer stepchildren; they are equal partners. On the basis of new conditions in world politics—and their own roles—it will be impossible in the future for either country to abdicate responsibility. Both have come of age.

The possible courses of action for both countries would seem to be different, however. West Germany can develop an active *Westpolitik* (Western policy) by incorporating European considerations in the restructuring of its partnership with the United States. Japan, of course, stands alone since it cannot advance along a similar political track in Asia. West Germany can help to settle the United States demand for a sharing of defense burdens along European lines. In this area in the Far East, Japan, again, stands on its own.

Nevertheless, what Japan does is of much greater significance to other Asian powers than the impact of the actions of West Germany on its West European neighbors. The directions of Japan's decisions will have important effects on such states as South Korea, the Philippines, Indonesia, and Thailand, and will influence the whole of United States policy towards Asia.

The Great Coup—Nixon's New China Policy

It was a novice who represented the United States in the United Nations when the question of Red China's admission and the exclusion of Taiwan came up for the last time. The policy which Ambassador George Bush articulated for the United States was new as well. In the early sixties, the conservative Texan had still explained: "If Red China is to be admitted to the United Nations, then the UN is finished, and we should withdraw." Ten years later, the same man representing the new United States policy spoke in favor of Red China's admission to the UN. This was a complete turnabout in a long-standing American attitude regarding China after all the years of bitterness between the two countries. It was not just the *fact* of a change in the American outlook on Red China; it was the *tempo* of the American-Chinese rapprochement that startled the world. It was almost like watching a magician in action—"Now you see it; now you don't."

As early as February 1971, Nixon clearly expressed his desire for this change in a speech before Congress: "We are ready to undertake a dialogue with Peking." Washington began talking of the "People's Republic of

China," in contrast to past diplomatic custom when it referred to "Mainland China" or "Communist China." Certainly calling a country by its proper name could be classified as an overture. Still, the United States did not want to abandon the interests of its ally, Taiwan, as shown by its continued defense support of that country. (Between 1951 and 1965, economic aid worth $1.5 billion had been provided to Taiwan.) But if it was to encourage any kind of rapprochement with Communist China, it was also clear that the United States had to abandon Taiwan's claim that it spoke for all of China. (This step, incidentally, was reminiscent of the approach of the Brandt administration in its surrender of the claim as sole representative of Germany in order to achieve normalization of relations with the German Democratic Republic [East Germany, referred to hereafter as GDR]. It seems characteristic of modern international politics that the rigid positions that developed during the years after World War II in the confrontation between the Free World and Communism are being diplomatically softened under the catchword of "normalization.")

The United States had set up extraordinarily solid barriers against Red China. Even freedom of movement, so highly valued by Americans, was severely limited. American passports contained the following notice: "Not valid for Mainland China." Travel to China was explicitly conditioned on official approval. At the same time, even as American travel restrictions began to be eased, the Chinese showed no interest in the prospect of visitors from the United States. In 1970, the total number of Americans who wanted to visit Red China numbered one thousand, but Red China granted visas to only three Americans. It would be hard to imagine more minimal contact between two world powers with a combined population of almost one billion.

Then the ping-pong ball went flying. In connection with the World Championship Games in Japan in 1971, the national table tennis team of the United States was offered a surprise invitation to meet for "friendly competition" in China. The American players were given a welcome by Mao Tse-tung that went far beyond that usually accorded visiting athletes from whatever country. Then seven American journalists were allowed to travel in China for the first time in twenty-two years. In an atmosphere of "ping-pong diplomacy," President Nixon took the lead immediately in lifting a number of U.S. restrictions on trade, shipping, currency and travel in order to improve relations between the two countries.

Nixon offered an indirect response to Mao Tse-tung. In a conversation with Edgar Snow, the China expert *par excellence* who had known both Mao and Chiang Kai-shek when both had been comrades-in-arms rather than enemies, Mao stated he would welcome a visit of an American President to China. For his part, President Nixon expressed the desire to go to China at some time in the near future. All of these are in fact marginal developments that gained meaning only after the sensational announcement of the secret Kissinger visit to Peking.

When Nixon appeared on national television on July 15, 1971, he announced the big surprise of that year in world politics. "Good evening. I have asked for time on television this evening in order to announce a major development in our search for a lasting peace in the world. As I have mentioned on several occasions during the last three years, there can be no stable and lasting peace without the participation of the People's Republic of China and her 750 million people. Therefore, I have taken the initiative in several spheres to open the door for normal relations between our two countries. . . . "

Nixon proceeded to report on Kissinger's visit and read the communiqué agreed upon by his foreign policy adviser and Chou En-lai to the effect that he himself would visit China "at an appropriate time before May 1972." The goal of the visit would be, he said, "the normalization of relations between the two countries and the exchange of ideas on questions of mutual interest."

President Nixon affirmed that this initiative was not directed against any nation in the world, and he stressed that the new relationship with the People's Republic of China should not be "at the expense of our old friends." With this remark Nixon intended to counteract from the very beginning the "inevitable speculations which are likely to follow this announcement."

Nixon's visit in February 1972 was the first ever made to China by a President of the United States. For the world it provided clear proof that China had stepped out of its own self-imposed isolation to play a role on the stage of world politics. (By this time, the People's Republic had already replaced Taiwan in the United Nations.) The final communiqué resulting from the Nixon visit summed up the conditions for normalization of relations and expressed hope for improved relations at all levels. Equally important were the pictures of the Nixon visit in Peking—and the live television coverage —seen around the world.

With this one bold stroke Nixon created a new style, a new form and rhythm, so to speak, for the international diplomacy of our day. His actions triggered a wave of traveling among statesmen and generated a rebirth of summitry. New life was breathed into the international political scene. And who knows, perhaps this side effect will be more important than the talking itself?

The normalization of relations between Washington and Peking will obviously be a long-term process, and the visit by President Nixon was only a beginning.

The basic aim of the People's Republic is, of course, to gain confirmation of its claim to sole representation of all China, including Taiwan. But as of now, this claim cannot be accepted by the United States. For this reason, the Kissinger trips to China in February 1973 resulted not in the establishment of formal diplomatic relations, but in the agreement to set up liaison offices in Peking and Washington. Although not classified as embassies, these offices will undoubtedly fulfill the essential functions of an embassy by dealing with trade questions and other matters.

Can these talks between the United States and China avoid having a bearing on the relationships of these two countries with the Soviet Union? Is it possible that these two powers will try to come to an agreement at the expense of the third?

The basic political motivation of the new American involvement with China, as conceived by Henry Kissinger, seems to be based on a kind of multipolar balance of power, which acknowledges the existence of China and replaces the old bipolar division between the United States and the Soviet Union. Under this Sino-Soviet-American triangle, China can continue to maintain its revolutionary image, while at the same time expanding its contacts with the West. It also provides the United States an opportunity to continue to work with the Soviet Union while expanding its relationships throughout the globe.

6

The Crisis of American Society

The turning point for the United States as a world power has been brought about by developments within American society. It has been from within the United States that doubts concerning the basic values of American foreign policy have been most clearly expressed. The war in Vietnam was not lost on the battlefields of that country, but rather within America itself. The disillusionment within American society about its own ability to realize self-declared goals for all Americans has had a profound effect on its foreign policy, too.

"Liberty," "justice for all"—and even affluence—the intangible best-selling exports of American foreign policy—seem to have faded into nothingness as Americans have turned inward to discover poverty in their midst and to find inequality throughout the system. The American Dream seems to have ended with a bang, not a whimper. As a result, distrust of American capabilities and intentions arose first in Asia and then spilled over to Europe.

The American image has lost its saintly status in the world. True, as indicated, America's best-selling export has always been its ideals—especially liberty. But unfortunately, in recent years, the image of the salesman has changed. People in many countries no longer see the United States as the great hope of the Free World. In their eyes, the American ideals have become tarnished. Certainly, Americans traveling abroad have sensed this reaction all around the world. For example, when an American in Moscow complained to a hotel doorman that his telephone wasn't working, the Russian retorted: "And what are you doing about your black people?"

The racial problem is the one single issue which has done the most to tarnish America's reputation abroad. In talking about the richest and most advanced country of the world, it seems that every general statement concerning American society must except one large segment of the population: the blacks. The events in America during the sixties must be credited with creating an awareness both inside and outside the United States that the country is sitting on a time bomb, and the time bomb is the racial problem. Even if the war in Vietnam and the unrest of the young people have only temporarily shaken American society, the racial problem will continue to dominate the domestic scene.

Eleven per cent of about 200 million Americans are black. America has had to admit that a major segment of its citizenry is condemned to life in undignified conditions, with little hope and future. Harlem, the black ghetto in New York, has become the symbol. But since every American metropolis has its Harlem, the solution of this American problem, unresolved for over a hundred years, is enormously difficult. During the postwar period, a part of the black population was able to rise to middle-class status and, particularly, into the upper strata. Today, about four times as many black people belong to the middle class as in 1945, but based on their roughly eleven per cent proportion of the total population they are still highly underrepresented in all higher strata.

In describing the situation of blacks in the United States, it is relevant to note that the average black earns less than the average white American and has inferior housing and education. Although his income rises more rapidly than that of the white American, there are no signs that the gap between the levels of blacks and whites will be closed in the foreseeable future.

During the presidential elections of the 1960's, black leaders tried to maneuver their constituencies into position as effective voting blocs in the campaigns in order to win improved living conditions. Kennedy based his narrow victory, and Johnson his windfall electoral success, on the support of blacks. Both attempted to answer the needs of American blacks: Kennedy, through the civil rights legislation, and Johnson, with the improvement of their social situation through government-sponsored programs in many areas. Yet neither attempt could decisively improve the situation.

In recent years, the racial problem has also seen regional changes and has because of this has entered even more into the awareness of the American consciousness. It is no longer a problem limited to the Southern states, but now concerns also the industrial areas on the East Coast around New York, in Michigan and Illinois, and finally in California. And in these highly industrialized areas, the racial problem has shown itself to be more and more an explosive force. The urban problem becomes more critical each year as new ghettos are established or old ghettos spread when whites leave for suburbia and exurbia and poor blacks take their places in the inner city. Blacks make up the majority of the poor, and they are afflicted by each national economic crisis to a disproportionate degree. They are hit harder than other groups by unemployment and inflation. Experience shows that the proportion of blacks among the unemployed in any region is usually double that of the white population.

America is faced with the danger that the racial problem might split the country into two societies and two cultures. What is happening in the United States in microcosm simply reflects what is happening in the world. This dichotomy between rich and poor, whites and blacks, industrially advanced and underdeveloped is already seen on the global stage in the contrast between rich and poor nations. This parallel image puts the problem clearly in its world political dimensions: Will the black ghettos become the beachhead of a Third World ready to fight the industrial nations—a beachhead inside the most developed and strongest industrial society on the globe?

In December 1970, Edgar Snow had a talk with Chairman Mao. At that time Mao thought a revolution in the United States would be impossible, but he also expressed the hope that a revolutionary party might develop in America. The economic, political and social situation of the blacks has already led to some movement, but most blacks have not supported, up to this time at least, such revolutionary groups. Unless conditions for blacks improve, however, America may find it difficult to prevent a mushrooming of this movement, which might be encouraged from outside the United States.

Closely linked to the racial problem is the increase in crime in the United States. In the big cities, crime is an everyday affair. Americans hear daily of criminal assaults in which their friends have been victims or of friends who have had their apartments burglarized. Many feel insecure in the large cities and are afraid to walk the streets at night.

There are many reasons for the drastic increase in crime and violence in the United States. Certainly drug addiction is a major cause. For example, official estimates are that eighty per cent of all robberies are committed by drug addicts, black and white, and since the proportion of drug addicts among the black population would seem to be higher than that among the white population, it is reasonable to assume that a higher proportion of blacks are involved in crime than whites. It is certainly true that the black ghettos have been subject to more crime than white neighborhoods, although crime in America has spread at such a rapid rate that it is reaching alarming proportions now even in its suburbs.

The wave of violence and crime provides evidence of the disorder of American society. This condition is not peculiar to the United States. Violence and crime are increasing in many parts of the world. The president of the Federal Bureau for Crime Investigation in West Germany fears a similar upsurge in the next few years. A basic problem for the American government is how to deal with such crime, and this in turn has raised a question about the nature of the society itself.

There are those who have said that the permissive society which has developed in the U.S. in recent years has been characterized by an excessive liberal tolerance which has opened the door to violence and crime. During the Presidential campaign of 1968, Nixon, for example, charged the existing Democratic administration with such permissive policies and cited it as responsible for the wave of crime and violence. Nixon ran his campaign on a law-and-order issue. In his administration, the

President has attempted to launch an all-out, determined effort against crime.

The danger of the law-and-order approach is evident, however. Government overemphasis on force as a deterrent in this area can lead to increased brutality by criminals and at the same time also runs the danger of violating the constitutional protections guaranteed all citizens, including those accused of crimes.

The critics of this policy ask themselves whether the progress America has made as a constitutional state might be lost in an overzealous pursuit of the criminal. Escalation of crime or law and order—or both—threaten to undermine the American constitutional system which has provided the basis of American democracy and a long-standing model for the world. Questions about the quality of life in American industrial society have also been raised. Are competition and achievement the be-all and end-all of American society? Is it right that a double standard for private and corporate ethics should exist? Can "technology at any cost" in all realms of life be called "progress"? Can expenditures for such technological triumphs as the moon landing be justified in terms of needs at home? Does the United States have a right or responsibility to fight a war like that in Vietnam when that war takes attention away from problems at home? Can the United States exist as a free society when there is racial injustice?

A portion of the country's youth has risen in revolt and articulated their concerns on these and other questions before the country, at the same time raising the consciousness level in the minds of other generations of Americans. While the political and private forms of protest among America's youth are constantly changing, the questions about the quality of life in an industrial society have remained. The students have been saying:

Change our society or it will destroy itself. Despite fears of the Establishment, no lasting Marxist or even neo-Marxist revolt has resulted, and peace has returned to the universities. But the catalytic role of the youth movement has remained, for it has illuminated a basic truth: One should not simply accept developments within the industrial society without question. And this truth, perhaps neglected, has been seized upon by many "thinking" Americans.

Having achieved the most advanced industrial society in the world and a position in the world as an international political power, Americans are now confronted by the need for coming to grips with their problems and America's role in the world. They are questioning the validity of their institutions, including the great powers of the presidency. They are examining closely the quality of individual life. They are searching for new approaches to the shared societal life. They are seeking a new sense of self-awareness.

All of this is not just a superficial philosophical discussion, for the questions are deeply embedded in contemporary America. The racial question, poverty, violence, drug addiction, urban ills, and environmental pollution are all problems which must be dealt with—and solved—immediately. For if they cannot be solved, what is America's potential as a viable society?

Will Americans be capable of coming to terms with their domestic problems? The answer depends on what one is looking at—the problems or the Americans. Whoever analyzes the problems must be skeptical of their prospects for solution. On the other hand, he who is familiar with Americans and their ability to solve their problems over the long run will trust them to live up to the challenge.

7

The Role of West Germany
As a Medium-Sized Power

West Germany must recognize that it is an independent state. It should also want to be one. Only by having a sense of its own identity can West Germany equip itself with the foundations for the kind of foreign policy necessary in its relations with its allies as well as with the Eastern European states.

Discussion about our role in world politics has been hampered because we have tended for too long to see West Germany only in the context of the question of German unity. For this reason, with one eye always looking towards reunification, we have considered West Germany only as a provisional arrangement, as a temporary thing. We kept thinking that we could not be "whole" until reunification took place. But this attitude is not adequate for the 1970s. New developments on the international scene require that we take a new look at who we are and what we are and where we are going.

To hold its own in light of contemporary developments in world politics and also to gain its own international objectives, West Germany must conceptualize its *raison d'état* in more precise terms. The country must strengthen itself domestically and must approach international affairs as an independent state. While it is true that West Germany had a dream—a united Germany, it also has had a reality—a movement toward its own identity. Developments in international politics since World War II seemed to allow no other alternative. According to German Professor Waldemar Besson, "from the very beginning, even if its leaders had not yet realized it, the Federal Republic (West Germany) was on the way to itself." It was the coalition of the Social Democratic Party (SPD) and the Free Democratic Party (FDP) in 1969 that first accepted this fact of political life and made it official policy. The policy statement of the new government in 1969, the Moscow and Warsaw treaties which followed, and the recent conclusion of the Basic Treaty with the GDR have put this policy into effect. But one must go back to the administration's statement of October 28, 1969, to understand the fine points of the approach. "That the Federal Republic [West Germany] should recognize the GDR as a sovereign state is out of the question. Even if two states exist in Germany, they can nevertheless not be foreign to each other. Their relations to each other can only be of a special kind." The government thus availed itself of an "out" that would preclude formal recognition, but at the same time would establish a modus vivendi: two German states in one German nation.

There is no need to go into details of international law on the legal aspects of inter-German relations. They have been defined by the government of West Germany as domestic German relations. What is important is that countries around the world have understood these terms. Brandt's *Ostpolitik* has provided them with a rationale for recognition of the GDR. The readiness of the present West German government to acknowledge formal international recognition of East Germany by other states is the end result of West Germany's ability to give up a rigid position to accept only a reunified Germany. For example, the Hallstein Doctrine (establishing that there should be no diplomatic relations between West Germany and those countries maintaining relations with East Germany) has finally been dropped as the guideline for German foreign policy. And the claim to sole representation—West Germany's insistence on being the legitimate spokesman for the whole of Germany—has been given up in the same process. Yet, long-held policies die hard. As late as September 25, 1968, a bipartisan statement of the German Bundestag still claimed: "Our allies and the vast majority of the nations of the world have made it known that they recognize the government of the Federal Republic [West Germany] as the only German government established under free and legal circumstances. This government speaks as well for those to whom full political participation has been denied up to this time. Diplomatic recognition of the other part of Germany as a foreign state or as a second sovereign state of the German nation cannot be taken into consideration."

During the early postwar period, West Germany representing in fact only a fragment of prewar Germany, maintained the legal point of view that the German nation with its 1937 boundaries should eventually be reconstituted. Support was given on this point by the Allies. The German nation had been broken down into five parts. First, there was the northern section of East Prussia, which was under Soviet administration and subject to final decision in a general peace treaty. Second, and under similar conditions, the former German provinces beyond the Oder-Neisse line as well as a part of

Pomerania fell under Polish administration. The third part was the Soviet Occupation Zone, which was obliged to consider itself the German Democratic Republic. The fourth part was the area of greater Berlin, subject to four-power occupation (France, Great Britain, U.S.S.R., and the United States) and belonging to neither the GDR nor West Germany. Finally, there was West Germany itself.

In the treaties concluded by West Germany with the Soviet Union and Poland, it abandoned any rights it may have wanted to assert relating to territorial questions and instead accepted the status quo. In doing so, the Government, in effect, made a major concession in its claim to a reconstituted German nation with its 1937 boundaries. As a result, the existence of West Germany itself began to seem less provisional and more permanent.

Yet, apart from this acceptance of the status quo, there are two principles of past policy on the German question that have remained unchanged.

First of all, no one seriously doubts that a majority of the whole population of all of Germany wants the reestablishment of national unity. The statements of all political parties as well as the reactions of the population clearly support this aim of West Germany. What the population in the other part of Germany thinks, no one can say with certainty. The neurotic concern among East German Communists for the image of their state certainly leads to the conclusion that they have not been successful in their attempt to transform those citizens of Germany into citizens of the German Democratic Republic. There is no reason to give the Communists the benefit of the doubt. They could demonstrate in a free election the extent to which the population of the GDR is no longer interested in a reunited Germany.

Second, related to the above is the necessity for self-determination for all Germans. While this principle is clearly expressed in Article Two of the Basic Treaty with the GDR in accordance with the United Nations Charter, the current government of West Germany was not able to include it directly in the treaties with Moscow and Warsaw. At the signing of the Moscow Treaty on August 12, 1970, the position of West Germany was, however, expressed in an accompanying note. "This treaty does not stand in contradiction to the political aim of the Federal Republic of Germany to work toward a condition of peace in Europe in which the German people will regain its unity through free self-determination." On the occasions of the ratification of the Moscow and Warsaw Treaties, all three political parties represented in the Bundestag confirmed the right of all Germans to self-determination in a joint resolution. This resolution was explicitly directed toward the treaty partners. It would be difficult to imagine, therefore, that the Soviet Union, the main treaty partner in the case of *Ostpolitik*, could believe that the German question has been permanently solved.

For its part, the government of West Germany believed that the appropriate reaction from the Soviet Union had been given in the remarks of Soviet Foreign Minister Gromyko regarding the Moscow Treaty: "The third point on which we have found each other in agreement relates to the future prospect of the reunification of Germany. Your position is clear, as is ours. We, too, have our own conception of how future unity will be achieved, and we could not make a treaty that ruled out all plans for the reunification of Germany. Under such circumstances, every comment concerning reunification would stand in contradiction of the treaty."

The question of self-determination naturally goes

to the very heart of the German question: the freedom of the German people. After World War II, only West Germany had the opportunity to choose its forms of state and government freely. The GDR, by contrast, had to accept a Communist dictatorship, as did the other nations of Eastern Europe. Since that time, West Germany and the GDR have had to confront each other as advocates of differing political and social systems: West Germany as the advocate of a free and democratic Germany, the GDR as the advocate of a Communist Germany.

Many Western allies continue to regard the German question as an important foreign policy issue, particularly in light of Brandt's *Ostpolitik*. It is often made clearer in these countries than in Germany itself that the German question has not disappeared simply because reunification remains unrealized after twenty-eight years. This is an additional reason why West Germany cannot retreat from the German question, even if it does see itself as a separate, independent state. So long as the claims of the GDR continue to point up the German question, it would be foolish for West Germany to leave the question to the Communists alone. It is true the Communists are hardly in a position today to become very aggressive about the reunification issue. While they are fighting doggedly to set themselves off from West Germany, it would seem that such efforts at delimitation might well backfire and instead develop a sense of community.

According to reports, the Socialist Unity Party (the Communist party in the GDR) has attempted to develop a "socialist German national culture" in the GDR, in which the history of Germany as a nation ends with the establishment of two states. This self-portrayal, which often embraces Prussian characteristics almost to a point of caricature, has surely been meant to provide grounds for an eventual campaign for German unity. Nevertheless, at present delimitation is the predominant policy.

The last word with regard to the German question has by no means been spoken. For this reason, West Germany will continue to demand self-determination for the citizens of the other Germany. Self-determination by the population of the GDR could result in one of two possible developments—the unity of the German nation or the definite establishment, based on the will of the people, of two German states. Naturally, either one of these choices, if based on true self-determination, would be respected by West Germany.

In any case, West Germany's call for the right of self-determination by the people of the GDR has had an effect on its own foreign policy. Clearly, self-determination is distinct from annexation, and when West Germany calls for self-determination, it certainly cannot be accused of applying power politics simply to incorporate the GDR. It, in fact, acknowledges the existence of GDR as a separate entity, providing a basis for the participation of both German states in the United Nations. Such a policy would also seem to be much more likely to be accepted by the countries of Eastern Europe: that people should decide for themselves how they wish to live politically and with whom they wish to come together.

The demand for self-determination is also compatible with our alliances with the West. As in the case of every policy directed toward the German problem, the question has been raised as to how far our allies and friends in the world are ready to support our point of view. Clearly, Adenauer had the commitment of the Western powers to the reunification of Germany in the treaties he concluded with the West. Upon the completion of the treaties with Moscow and Warsaw, Brandt also received explicit confirmation of support in a communiqué from the NATO states dated December 8, 1972. NATO supports our demand for the right to self-determination for all Germans.

Adenauer's ordering of his political priorities was first freedom, then peace, and then unity. Without doubt, this sequence contributed substantially to the realization of what was possible and also what was feasible in the postwar period—the establishment of West Germany as a liberal and socially enlightened democracy. Heinrich von Brentano, Foreign Minister under Adenauer, was clearly referring to this point when he said: "We cannot gain assurance of the reunification of Germany if we begin by surrendering the security of the Federal Republic [West Germany]." These words spoken in the Bundestag in March of 1958 are still true today.

The preamble of our constitution contains a mandate to pursue unity and freedom. But it is even more significant that the outline of the constitution preceding the preamble presents the basis for the first viable democracy ever to have existed in Germany. The duration of this democracy already speaks for its stability. Consider the arithmetic. It has been in existence for twenty-eight years since World War II; that is as long a period as from the year 1945 back to the Russian Revolution in 1917. After twenty-eight years, however, not only was the Weimar Republic already dead, but the Hitler dictatorship had gone under as well.

West Germany was established under the hallmark of freedom. It has developed a liberal order which it can defend and improve. It wants these freedoms for the other Germans as well. Our freedom tied to social and economic progress has been a source of political strength from which West Germany has derived its dynamic way of life. This remains the case even when freedom is blurred by the everyday circumstances of an industrial society, and sometimes even if it is lost and must be regained.

It is when one compares two systems—one in which people have this freedom and one in which they do not—that one sees the German question must continue to be kept alive. It will be the task of West Germany to see to it that our freedom has a future.

New Tasks in the West and in the East

West Germany must recognize the validity of its own existence by affirming that the integrity of its liberal system is worthy of defense. Through such a step, the secret hopes of the Communists can be frustrated.

The Eastern world has been revising the current form of its ideology in every domain with the aim of bringing it back again in a different form. It must be realized, however, that even in the interests of good relations with Communist states, no such new form could lead West Germany ever to accept any modifications or any changes in its system. West Germany could accept the territorial status quo in the interest of peace in Europe. But the Soviet Union must recognize that Germany will forgo a peace on Soviet terms if it threatens to destroy the freedom of German democracy. The foreign policy of Bonn must oppose an extension of the Brezhnev Doctrine to include West Germany.

West Germany is a medium-sized power, as are

Canada, South Africa, Italy, and Japan. India, Argentina, and Brazil belong to a similar category. These are countries that have not achieved world power status for a variety of reasons including, of course, their lack of nuclear weapons. Nevertheless, they are powers which, because of a number of factors, have been assigned important roles in world affairs distinct from those of the smaller nations. One would also have to include Great Britain and France among these medium-sized powers because their nuclear potentials are only of minimal military significance. But the medium-sized powers of Europe have a chance of climbing to the world power level of the Soviet Union, China, or the United States. Political integration of Western Europe is the way in which this goal may be achieved.

One can discuss medium-sized powers in current international affairs in terms of the continuing changes in the relations between the great powers, which have switched back and forth from conditions of total confrontation to mere antagonism to cooperation. One reason for this has been the technological rivalry and the resulting gap that has developed between the world powers and the rest of the globe. In fact, concern that the world powers might cooperate at the expense of all other countries and a fear that the technological lead of the giants could only increase the gap between rich and poor nations have spurred the medium-sized powers to become more active in international politics once again.

West Germany is such a medium-sized power. Above all, the power of the country's economic potential gives it a position of great significance in world trade. Furthermore, the location of the country between two of the major world powers adds to its particular importance in the international system. But medium-sized powers do not make world politics, and this is true for

West Germany as well. It is not the intention nor within the capability of West Germany to roam the great open spaces; Europe is the center of its interest. Germany must attempt to maximize its diplomatic leverage in this region, always remaining aware that developments in another part of the world might quickly limit the prospects for its local diplomatic efforts.

This emphasis on Europe is reminiscent of Bismarck. He once disagreed with supporters of a foreign policy of colonialism for Germany by stressing the importance of the country's strategic position between Russia and France in order to show the limited relevance of African territory. Bismarck's point of view should remind West Germany that it is not only a medium-sized power but also a state in the middle of Europe. At the moment, it is true that this middle position marks a boundary, but we still hope that there will some day be more permeable borders at the center of Europe once again. Along with Bismarck, Gustav Stresemann comes to mind as a symbolic figure for the current West German foreign policy even though he was never able to bring to an end the *Ostpolitik* that he had planned. One can conclude in general that a greater effort is once again under way. In fact, it already began during the Adenauer era under Foreign Minister Gerhard Schröder.

West Germany is typical of today's medium-sized power in attempting to take advantage of the developing multipolarity to achieve an independent foreign policy. Like all medium-sized powers, Germany has an interest in minimizing tensions between the Soviet Union and the United States. In its own case, it is immediately affected by any level of strain between the super powers over West Berlin. The situation is no setting for a self-satisfied, idyllic existence.

But West Germany is a liberal, democratic, and

constitutional state, and it wishes to remain such. Its international goal is to surmount the division of the whole of Europe through Western European integration and thus to create a partner of equal weight to the United States. It will not give up its aim of making self-determination possible for the people of the GDR. West Germany has resolved upon the following foreign policy goals during the next decade: freedom throughout Germany, unity and balance in Europe, cooperation in the Atlantic Alliance, and aid for the Third World. While West Germany can do a great deal on its own to assure its domestic freedom, it remains in need of foreign backing for its security today as it has in the past. This backing is provided above all by the United States.

For most of the European states, a politically integrated continent could lessen or even eliminate this condition of dependence. But as long as that goal has not been achieved, our partnership with the United States will remain indispensable to the security of West Germany. Furthermore, with regard to future progress in the highly developed industrial economy of West Germany, stimuli from the United States will remain as vital as ever on the basis of America's technological lead.

European Integration and Atlantic Partnership

It is of the utmost importance that West Germany avoid what could be a major misunderstanding. Just because it is located between East and West does not mean that it can be transformed into a neutral power. By such a move, the country's newly won flexibility could easily be lost. In such a situation, West Germany might fall under the influence of the Soviet Union. Therefore, it must continue to concentrate its energies on its relations with the West. Even if it is possible today to pursue both *Ostpolitik* and *Westpolitik* at the same time, the focal point of German foreign policy for the seventies lies in the West. If West Germany wishes to remain free, secure, and independent, it must participate in the resolution of international political questions concerning the future of Europe. It must stand up for a policy by which Western Europe will remain in the American sphere of influence. These states must resist falling under the sway of the Soviets, so that they—with political systems based on democracy—can maintain their freedom of action.

West Germany surely must be conscious of its increased significance in this confrontation. There is no doubt that the country looms large in the calculations of the Soviet Union. True, the Soviet Union has accepted, for the moment, the fact that West Germany is a part of the Western alliance system and is firmly anchored to the European Common Market. The gentlemen in the Kremlin surely have come to the conclusion that West Germany cannot be drawn out of these alliances in any short period of time. They are trying, therefore, to tempt German policy with a different appeal. The Soviet leaders have suggested to West Germany that it could gain what de Gaulle strove to achieve for France. They have offered Germany a position as the privileged Western partner of the Soviet Union. Above all, the Soviet Union would be delighted if West Germany were to turn away from the Western efforts geared to achieving the political unification of Europe and the strengthening of the German-American alliance. Success by the Soviet Union in the achievement of these goals could mean a recognition of the status quo in Europe and the assurance of continued Soviet control of its territorial possessions gained at the end of World War II. One can hardly imagine that this would be the last phase of the Soviet policy for Europe. It can be said with certainty that the Soviet Union has tied its hopes to hindering the political unification of Europe and to the prospect that, as a consequence of this development, the United States would then be induced to terminate its involvement in Europe. Britain's entrance into the Common Market can only have momentarily subdued these aspirations.

The style of this new Soviet policy is being formed through a multitude of undramatic decisions on details in the generally more comfortable political climate of Europe today. Public opinion in the nations of Western Europe is widely sympathetic toward détente with the Soviets. In fact, in the current context of East-West rapprochement this strategy has become the basis for public hopes.

Brandt's new *Ostpolitik* is celebrated in West Germany as a foreign policy of change. It is supposed to lead to détente in Europe. West Germany is seen as the bridge-builder between East and West, overcoming the hardened postures of both sides. One cannot miss a certain exuberance in these *Ostpolitik* initiatives that is reminiscent of the mood of a youth movement. But at the same time these initiatives set other developments into motion, developments which could threaten our policies and especially our domestic way of life. In the enthusiasm for *Ostpolitik*, some of its possible consequences have been completely overlooked. The bridge to be built may, in effect, become a one-way street by which the Soviet Union gains access to Western Europe, while we continue to remain standing before the impermeable boundaries of the Eastern bloc. The Soviet concept of peace still suggests to us that a reduction of tensions is also tied to a reduction of freedom.

West Germany cannot and should not conceal its origin and the implications of that origin. It grew out of developments in international politics in which the two world powers, each with a distinct political approach to life, collided with each other. The search for the right political system defined its function in the East-West conflict. German foreign policy, in fact, has become a barometer for assessing the political weather conditions at any given moment in the East-West relationship. Waldemar Besson has seen a kind of subsystem of bipolar international politics in West Germany. He has characterized it as "the first and most important subsystem of the Cold War."

But a few things have happened in this subsystem. Since World War II ended, we have become "somebody" again, as Chancellor Erhard announced as early as 1965. On the other hand, West Germany has also been characterized as a giant in economic affairs but a dwarf in foreign affairs. Since then the country's view of itself has come to oscillate less and less between dwarf and giant. Under no conditions does the subsystem want to be in line in the pecking order of countries that some other country has set for it. West Germany must find its own place in line. It must attempt to serve God without angering the devil. It must continue to pursue *Westpolitik* while it also seeks arrangements with the East. It seems logical that the more progress that is made in the former, the greater the security with which the latter can be applied.

West Germany's Western course was charted at its

birth. It had two components from the beginning: one American and the other West European. Both served the causes of security and freedom. The tie to the United States has guaranteed the security and freedom of West Germany and West Berlin has proved itself. This has been a success of lasting importance, even though the goal of reunification has not been achieved. The brunt of the burden of this guarantee has been carried by the United States, and over the years the burden has become heavier for the Americans. On the basis of this changed situation, West Germany must help to strengthen the European component of its Western course. A politically unified Europe must become a partner of equal weight to the United States and support an equivalent contribution to the defense of a free Europe.

The chief aim of West Germany for the seventies is to make progress towards its major goal—the political unification of Europe. It must be ready to play a leading role in developing European initiatives that will lead to this goal. And it must also see to it that every activity improves political cooperation within Europe and close cooperation between Europe and the United States. In this respect, again, the diplomatic leeway of West Germany has increased. First of all, a simple survival instinct leads to an active political role; it is the country most immediately affected by any sense of insecurity in the West. Because of its security interests, West Germany is the natural intermediary between the United States and Europe. Furthermore, West Germany has contributed an economic potential to the Common Market that is clear for all to see. And, equally important, its people strongly support its moves toward international cooperation. Finally, West Germany justifiably points out that the policies of détente which it supports along with the powers of the West can only be successful if the Western alliance remains a viable political reality. The questions related to the European Security Conference concerning mutual troop reductions in the East and the West can be dealt with only in this context.

We shall not be able to wage an *Ostpolitik* that defends our interests if we are not able to convince the United States of the necessity for it to continue playing a role in Europe, while at the same time encouraging greater West European efforts to help relieve the burden carried by the Americans. West Germany must fight to see that Europe makes its own contribution in accordance with the Nixon Doctrine. Our security, which has rested until now on the pillar of the United States, must now be placed on the second pillar of Western Europe.

Political unification of Europe is our goal. The series of complicated detailed decisions involved in the politics of Europe should not be allowed to distract us from the fact that the rest of the years of the decade of the seventies will decide whether Western Europe will remain merely a customs union or become a political community. A state cannot be allowed to think of its politics as some kind of international beauty contest. For this reason, West Germany must hold on to its demands for a united Europe, even when our Western neighbors are not always in complete agreement.

West Germany knows that its interests and its future are rooted firmly in the political unity of Europe. It sees a Europe in close partnership with the United States, supported by the common orientation of all the Western democracies to political and social progress. The Atlantic Alliance strengthens the security of Europe. Through common technological and scientific undertakings, it supports the development of Western industrial society. It is the positive basis for East-West détente in all of Europe. Unification of Europe's peoples, the strengthening of the Atlantic Alliance, and a modus operandi with the East—those are the political tasks West Germany must complete if it wishes to achieve the goals it has set for itself.

As years have gone by, the population of West Germany has come to feel more and more secure. This feeling of security has rested on two expectations with regard to the two superpowers: that the Soviet Union will not attack, and that the United States will defend us come what may. In light of the rapid change on the international scene, however, West Germany, through an active foreign policy of its own, must assure itself that these expectations are still realistic. The balance of power between the Western alliance and the Soviet bloc that guarantees our security is not a natural condition. The balance might at any moment be altered as a result of the international political problems of the United States as well as by the expansion of Soviet influence, particularly in the Middle East and in the Mediterranean. West Germany would be the first victim of any new imbalance of power. Were the Soviet Union to be successful in establishing a new tilt in the plane of European politics, ours is the first state that would slide off in the direction of the East. For this reason, the priorities of West Germany's foreign policy should be designated to maintain the Western alliance at a sufficient level of strength to protect the present balance of power. The political will of West Germany is a dominant factor in European politics: If the country puts its full weight on the scale and presses with initiatives of its own, the Western alliance will remain strong enough to maintain the balance of power. This sense of responsibility for the well-being of the Western alliance has developed parallel to West Germany's new self-image as an independent state.

Domestic Polarization over Questions of Foreign Policy: A Shot That Backfires

On June 30, 1960, Herbert Wehner, then Vice Chairman of the SPD and the opposition spokesman in the German Parliament, stepped in front of the microphone to announce that his party had agreed to the principle of a bipartisan foreign policy. After eleven years of opposition to the politics of Adenauer, the Social Democratic Party accepted the treaty system behind West Germany's integration with the West. Wehner was saying, in effect, that in the event of the establishment of a Social Democratic government, these treaty commitments would be respected and maintained. Will a similar scene be repeated in the seventies? Will Carl Carstens, the parliamentary leader of the Christian Democratic Union, or some other CDU politician announce that Brandt's system of treaties with the East will be accepted in a similar fashion? Or will Brandt be forced to admit, after the shifts he has stimulated in international politics, that the balance sheet of his *Ostpolitik* has gone into the red?

These scenes are reminiscent of Saul on the road to Damascus. They are the typical result of premature polarization with regard to questions of foreign policy. When the Brandt administration took office, the battle scenes from the early years of West Germany repeated themselves with the roles reversed. In both cases, the opposition grew rigid through a policy of radical criticism.

Around 1815, a *Dictionnaire de Girouettes* was published anonymously in Paris. This "lexicon of weather vanes" listed in alphabetical order the men in French political life who had switched their political convictions in the course of the international political currents of the early nineteenth century. Beside each name, a little flag was printed for each change of opinion. For most, there were many little flags. One often has the impression with regard to the scene in Bonn that such an index might be needed by the parliamentary leaders there to keep track of the many shifts by our own political leaders. Johannes Gross, the well-known West German journalist and political writer, has commented on the confusion in the current parliamentary scene.

> Confrontation should above all promote a constructive delineation of the two opponents. Current conditions of confrontation between the contending camps in German politics can suggest misleading and superficial differences. One party appears only too quickly to recognize the international status quo with self-satisfaction at its good deeds, while it remodels the domestic scene following a hodgepodge of ideological recipes. The other seems only to follow hesitatingly and with a sullen face. Instead, we should see one great party of permanent reform confronted by another that stands for the defense of the legal foundations of our liberal constitutional state.

Apart from these considerations of party tactics, there is a most important and profound feature rooted in the history of West Germany. On two occasions, governments felt obliged to pursue first *Westpolitik* and then *Ostpolitik* without any chance of achieving reunification, the main goal of the German people. On both occasions, the policy of the government was attacked assiduously by the opposition. The characterization of Adenauer by Kurt Schumacher, first chairman of the SPD in the post-World War II period, as the "Allies' Chancellor" reflected the bitterness of those days. The Christian Democratic opposition of today has not taken up the same tone, but the resoluteness of its position comes close to that of the Social Democratic Party in the former instance. The conditions of confrontation today are manifest particularly in electoral campaigns and in the debates in the German Parliament. Through all of its decisions, the Christian Democratic Union has confirmed its basic readiness for experimentation with *Ostpolitik*. In fact, it was only because of the abstention of the CDU that the Moscow and Warsaw treaties were ratified in the German parliament. In the same sense, the CDU supported the treaty on the regulation of traffic that was concluded between West Germany and the German Democratic Republic. But this still did not keep the *Ostpolitik* debates from being reminiscent of those in the fifties.

If one were to exaggerate the goals of the two parties, one might be tempted to say that the CDU presents itself as the party of *Westpolitik*, the SPD as that of *Ostpolitik*. But this prevailing impression must be completely revised if one examines the statements and programs of both parties more carefully. In fact, the ruling party, the SPD, has pointed out, quite rightly, that the Western nations today expect West Germany to pursue an active *Ostpolitik*. Without doubt, the CDU has underestimated the depth of this sentiment.

On the other hand, the CDU has noted the waning stability of the Western alliance, which is clearly in a state of flux as a result of developments in both the United States and Europe. The assertion of the SPD that it has been building its *Ostpolitik* on the secure ground of Western alliances is false to the extent that serious efforts are needed at this point to maintain the stability of the Western ties.

An energetic effort is needed to support both European cooperation and the Atlantic partnership. Yet, the CDU must take care not to accept too readily the risks related to Brandt's *Ostpolitik*. Such risks are being taken by an all-too-willing readiness to accept Eastern interpretations of the political consequences of the treaties. Instead, we should resist Communist interpretations as firmly as we have in the past. It is certainly not always easy to keep one's composure when one views the *Ostpolitik* of the current government. The bases on which this government claims to have based its policies have obliged it to make concessions to the East that should make one pause for reflection.

Brandt has characterized the political unification of Europe as a task that cannot be completed in this generation. Certainly this assignment for Europe will take a long time. But the long-standing ideological reservation of the SPD with regard to the prospect of European integration, as it has evolved in the postwar years, is revealed in Brandt's remark. Furthermore, from the point of view of its domestic social and political goals, the SPD does not see that the time for compliance with the European idea has come. Does it see its *Ostpolitik* in terms of those social and political goals? Might the SPD even use *Ostpolitik* as a means to transform the society of West Germany? There are certainly such currents within the SPD.

For the present leadership of the party, *Ostpolitik* is a means of securing its position. It does not aim at turning the society of West Germany inside out through *Ostpolitik*. It wants to show by this policy the *raison d'être* and the capability for innovation in the new government. There are some among the SPD who see a direct relationship between *Ostpolitik* and the party's policies for social change in Germany, but this is not the point of view of the current leadership. The SPD wants first of all to be able to publicize in the international system the successes of its *Ostpolitik*. Its secondary concern is for domestic policy, and only then does it finally come to European questions. "But Europe cannot wait until the SPD believes it has achieved a satisfactory number of aims of its own party platform." This comment made by Richard von Weizsaecker, member of the Federal Executive Committee of the CDU, illustrates the grounds behind the demand of the CDU for an active policy towards Europe, which it feels is neglected by the present government.

The foreign policies of both large parties of West Germany have been numbed by a set of one-sided conclusions concerning the contemporary international political scene. The CDU sees the dangers of the *Ostpolitik*, but does not appreciate clearly enough the need for this policy in some form. For its part, the SPD overestimates the strength of the Western alliance and denies the urgency of political initiatives aimed at maintaining their viability.

The Federal Republic needs a unity of foreign policy which will attempt to tie its *Ostpolitik* together with a *Westpolitik*. It must learn to deal with the subtleties of international politics. The Nixon Doctrine was not initiated by Brandt, nor was the Brezhnev Doctrine first pronounced by Barzel. We cannot allow ourselves an orientation only toward the East because the United States has become less supportive. We cannot be oriented to the West alone because the Soviet Union still maintains its ambition for hegemony over Europe. A condition of antagonism between the current government of West Germany and the opposition has resulted from this polarization in the debate on foreign policy. But when political attitudes and initiatives are determined by extreme points of view, the capacity for deciding upon the right policy is usually impaired.

Isn't it curious that the CDU and the SPD often argue for extreme points of view in this controversy, while in fact they are competing for the middle? Party strategists in both camps know perfectly well that what may be gained in splinter-group support on the left or right is lost many times over in the middle. And the voter in the middle feels himself torn this way and that. Furthermore, all experience to date shows that the voter orients himself in his voting decision primarily on the basis of his own concrete economic and social situation.

This does not mean that the importance of foreign policy should be underestimated. Because of the changes in domestic social relationships that result from international developments, foreign affairs can have a major effect on the personal situation of the individual citizen. There can be no doubt that a tie existed between Adenauer's policies of integration with the West and his "social market economy."

The Brandt government is not planning any societal changes in the context of its *Ostpolitik*. The question must be raised, however, whether, after Brandt, the SPD will still be able to maintain the distinctiveness of its *Ostpolitik* from its domestic policy. The fact is that in a certain number of SPD minds the thought does flutter that the innovations of *Ostpolitik* might also lead to a new era in domestic affairs. Domestic political changes as a result of this foreign policy could be all the more likely if in the long run *Ostpolitik* is overemphasized and *Westpolitik* neglected.

Beyond all this, however, it must not be overlooked that the limits to the political alternatives open to West Germany demand a foreign policy showing both community and continuity.

In West Germany, a political situation must not be allowed to develop in which the hopes of the Soviet Union are pinned on one political party and those of the Americans and Europeans on the other. The foreign policy of West Germany will have more clout if the Brandt government can point to strong domestic opposition to its foreign policy approaches to gain a better bargaining position in its negotiations with the East. The government can strengthen its position in the West by gathering the support of the opposition in order to be able to act on a broad base of support in its political initiatives towards the United States and Europe. In fact, German foreign policy today can be built on a greater foundation of continuity than the Brandt government has been willing to admit. Détente politics existed under Erhard, Schröder, and Kiesinger. Schröder, and later the Kiesinger administration, undertook political initiatives in the East which met with success. The concept of the renunciation of force, on which a good portion of the current *Ostpolitik* is based, was first articulated in a note from the Erhard government as early as 1966. A policy for Europe has existed since the founding of West Germany. Adenauer initiated it. Ever since then, the peoples and politicians of Europe have had evidence of the readiness of the West Germany for European cooperation.

What is true for the current government regarding

continuity applies to the opposition with regard to its shared responsibility. It, too, must remember that it has already actively pursued and supported the concept of *Ostpolitik*. The opposition must soberly confirm the fact that *Ostpolitik* is necessary today and must analyze exactly which compromises it feels are acceptable, given the conditions of international affairs. It is important, in any case, that the domestic controversies over the foreign policy of West Germany do not disturb our trust in the United States. The discussion must not be allowed to continue in such a way that the SPD in the course of its *Ostpolitik* would lose faith in the United States or that the CDU should reject *Ostpolitik* for fear of the reaction of the Western alliance. Neither position would do justice to changing German-American relations or achieve a realistic basis for the continuation and the strengthening of the Western alliance system.

8

The German-American Alliance

While occasionally a love story, the German-American alliance has always been a success story. The extraordinary success of this alliance lies in its contribution to the domestic affairs of West Germany and in its defensive orientation towards foreign challenges. Democracy in West Germany came into being under the protection of the United States. It developed as a liberal order, socially enlightened and based on a strong economy. In foreign affairs, West Germany and particularly West Berlin, have remained secure from Soviet pressure. Thus Adenauer's policy of German-French reconciliation aroused concern just as Brandt's *Ostpolitik* does today. Both have been seen as novel departures in German policy. The German-American alliance, however, is not merely one aspect of modern German history but a decisive element as a result of its preeminent place in our politics. The alliance with the United States is an integral part of the West Germany: In effect, it provides a second constitution for our country. A state which claims to be liberal and socially enlightened must establish its society on the two basic preconditions of economic growth and security from foreign influence which might threaten the underlying values of this society. In their alliance with the United States, West Germans found the support that was necessary to fulfill both of these conditions.

At Harvard University, on June 5, 1947, Secretary of State George C. Marshall announced plans for a comprehensive program of American economic aid for Europe. This aid was offered to all the countries of Europe to relieve "hunger, poverty, desperation, and chaos." The states of Eastern Europe were forced by Stalin to refuse, even though Czechoslovakia, for one, had already decided to accept the American offer.

Soviet Foreign Minister Molotov argued curiously that the Marshall Plan proposals were unrealistic, given the then-current status of American domestic politics. On the basis of reasoning which has seen broader acceptance in the seventies than it promised in the forties, Molotov thought the foreign-aid program had little chance for passage in Congress.

But the Soviet Union itself contributed unwittingly to the ratification of the plan by large majorities in both houses of the American Congress. In February 1948, the Soviet Union showed the true nature of its European policy with the Communist takeover of Czechoslovakia. The argument comes up frequently today that the division of Europe was the result of World War II. Yet, it is important to remember that Europe became divided only after World War II ended and the Cold War began. In fact, it was the Soviets who consolidated this division, just as it was the Soviets who started the Cold War.

Meanwhile, the United States started the European Recovery Program (ERP), the so-called Marshall Plan. This program was conceived for the whole world, but it was particularly decisive in the reconstruction of Western Europe through the allocation of $13 billion. West Germany received $1.3 billion in Marshall Plan aid and an additional $2 billion in other forms, such as loans and credits for the purchase of goods or for payment of transport services.

The United States provided not only financial aid but also know-how. Technical consultation and research assistance were given within the framework of the technical-aid program. Up to that point, American aid to the West Germany had been particularly important in humanitarian fields. Theodor Heuss, the former President of West Germany, characterized this process as totally novel in world history. "Until May 8, 1945, the citizens of the United States had to pay high taxes for the destruction of the German state. After May 8, they had to pay in order to save the German people." Our country had been destroyed by bombs, and its factories had been flattened. Without such help it would hardly have recovered in the short time it did. Packages sent by CARE meant immediate relief for many people in great personal need. At a time when the Eastern Occupation Zone was weakened by the comprehensive dismantling policies of the Soviets, the Western zones had laid the foundation stone for reconstruction made possible through aid from the United States. By 1952, the Gross National Product had nearly doubled, compared to 1946. The German mark was traded again on the world monetary market as a stable currency. The "social market economy" and sustained economic growth were the distinguishing characteristics of the German economic miracle. Nowhere else in Europe was the success of American aid demonstrated so strikingly. The United States requested the repayment of only a small part of this total aid provided, as stipulated in the London Agreement of 1953. These demands on West Germany were fully covered by the German Federal Bank in 1961. The last installment on the debt was paid in the summer of 1971.

United States aid to West Germany was the basis for what might well be referred to as the honeymoon in German-American relations throughout the decade of the fifties.

The German alliance with the United States was of equal importance for the security of West Berlin. The attempt of the Soviet leadership to starve West Berlin by blockade was thwarted as a result of the successful American airlift of relief flights. Berlin became the symbol for the close German-American alliance. It has remained such a symbol to this day. United States involvement in West Berlin still demonstrates the determination of America to block Soviet expansion.

The American concept of the containment of Soviet expansionist ambitions in Europe is the heart of our alliance. For strategic and economic reasons, the United States is not willing to permit Europe to fall under the sway of a single power. This policy had already led to American involvement in two world wars and has defined United States policy in the postwar period. The United States showed a readiness to return to its traditional foreign policy in its plans to leave the Continent at the end of the war. Roosevelt assured Stalin at Yalta that American troops would be withdrawn within two years after the fighting in Europe had ended. This plan was already under way when the Soviet Union began to consolidate its satellite empire in Eastern Europe. The United States was forced to conclude that only its continued presence in Europe could save the Western European states from a similar fate. In this way, the German-American alliance was influenced from the beginning by an all-too-visible and aggressive third party in the East, the Soviet Union.

This situation remains unchanged today. But the climate and intensity of the German-American alliance are significantly affected by the attitude of the United States towards the Soviet Union. Through Berlin and through its geographic position as a state bordering immediately on the Soviet sphere of influence, West Germany is directly wired into the circuit of tensions between the two great powers. West Germany cannot engage in détente or Cold War policy without the support of the United States. This was one of the important lessons which German foreign policy-makers had to learn. At the end of the Adenauer era, Foreign Minister Gerhard Schroder was the outstanding politician in drawing the necessary conclusions for German foreign policy from these lessons. German policy could not oppose détente if the United States was pursuing it with the Soviet Union. This lesson of the sixties is closely connected with the developing Soviet-American stalemate. As the leading midwife at the birth of West Germany, the United States has always regarded its policy towards Germany as part of its policy towards the Soviet Union.

Yet this fact has also provided a basis for the self-confidence of West Germany, in spite of its dependence on the United States. It is an indispensable partner in the American policy of containment directed towards the Soviet Union. The incorporation of West Germany in the Soviet bloc would definitely disturb the European balance of power which the United States is so eager to uphold. Shared interest in this concern has engendered a decisive firmness in the German-American alliance up to the present. In the present period of transition from tension to détente in Europe, the German-American alliance provides the sole guarantee that West Germany will not slip into a sphere of influence that would endanger its liberal and socially concerned domestic development.

In the context of world politics, the fate of West Germany remains that of those countries that are marginal to the interaction of the great powers. Saigon is not Berlin, and Taiwan is not West Germany. The situations of Israel and South Korea are equally disparate from that of West Germany. But, undoubtedly, the security of these states in the current world situation cannot be conceived of apart from the totality of American defense commitments.

Sometimes it is argued that the United States dominates Western Europe to the same degree that the Russians dominate Eastern Europe. One hegemony is said to be no better or worse than the other. This is not only a dangerous comparison, but as undifferentiated as it is untrue. The main characteristic of Soviet hegemony is that it has established an imperial system of domination. Within its sphere, it tolerates only those political systems which are identical with Soviet Communism.

We need only remember that the statutes of the political parties in the Communist satellite states officially recognize the leading role of the Communist Party of the Soviet Union. The 1968 invasion of Czechoslovakia by the Warsaw Pact powers under the leadership of the Soviet Union demonstrated anew that the satellite countries are not allowed to discard their Communist order. Nor are these countries permitted to pursue an independent European policy in contrast to the Western European nations whose sovereignty is not infringed upon by the United States. The Brezhnev Doctrine, granting only limited sovereignty to the Soviet Union's satellites, continues to be effective in the Soviet bloc.

West Germany has never been a satellite of the United States. Certain guidelines were laid down by the Allies, but these gave way to processes of independent self-development. In comparing the German Democratic Republic to West Germany, we can contrast the effects of Soviet and American hegemony on domestic politics. In fact, the two Germanys are comparable only in the formal terms of world politics. Each is an important ally of one of the two leading powers, the United States and the Soviet Union. Were either Germany to leave its respective camp, a considerable or even decisive disturbance of the balance of power would result.

This is the crucial reason why the leading goal of the German-American alliance—the reunification of Germany—cannot be achieved. With the construction of the Berlin Wall in 1961, this fact became clear. This development was a consequence of the balance of terror, resulting from the atomic stalemate at the end of the fifties. The United States had the will but lacked the power to realize the wish of the Germans for reunification. It was the only World War II ally in the Western alliance unhesitatingly to adopt Adenauer's goal of reunification. Because of its size and power, the United States had no reason to fear a unified Germany. In this, it differed from Germany's European neighbors, which understandably saw this goal from a very skeptical point of view.

The stated intention of the United States to defend democracy in the world and the support of this intention by West German policy formed the essential element of an alliance which otherwise would have lacked a clear *raison d'être*. While West Germany grew to the position of a medium-sized power under the protection of the NATO alliance, it was initially a weak and divided state facing a United States at the zenith of its strength. Could a German politician in Washington at that early time have done other than to embrace the aim of the Western alliance to preserve the order of freedom in the world? Since then additional factors have promoted further harmony between these two allies.

But is it possible for a medium-sized power and a world power to cooperate? We have also seen that, although there is more leeway in international relations for medium-sized powers today, limits are still set by the bipolar predominance of the United States and the Soviet Union. Second-strike capability in a nuclear conflict is the whip-hand of the two world powers. The Chinese still lack this capacity. Furthermore, a world power today should be a country with a population of at least 150 million, and it should cover at least 7 million square miles. Another indicator of world power status is a Gross National Product that exceeds $200 billion. These indicators emphasize the gaps between West Germany and the United States.

During our period of reconstruction and, above all, in the progressive development of our modern industrial society, we have been exposed to many dynamic impulses from the United States, the major one of which, of course, has been economic. French journalist Jean-Jacques Servan-Schreiber has depicted the U.S. economic challenge to all Western European states in his book, *The American Challenge*. His ideas are not greatly at variance with the conceptions of Paul Valéry, who predicted a future era in which an American commission would administer Europe. Our own view of the German-American alliance is above all in terms of protection and security. Yet, our relationship to the United States is more than a security alliance. We were aided by American science, technological know-how, and modern methods of management in order to close the gap created by the Hitler period, and to catch up quickly with the mainstream of progress in the West. Our élite leadership during the postwar period has been influenced intellectually by theories developed at Stanford, Berkeley, and Harvard. Many of those who had been to the United States in the fifties raved about the country of unlimited opportunities.

Another dynamic impulse has been the "American way of life" which has been introduced into everyday German life. This has been most evident in the field of entertainment, where hit films, music, plays, and so on from the United States have dominated the scene. But it has also been true of American fashion, household products, furnishings, and so on. We are frequently told by foreign observers that the Germans have become typical Americans, in fact, more American than Americans themselves. There have, of course, been critics of this Americanization process. Many, however, have failed to differentiate between Americanization and industrialization. What we have adopted from the United States are the developments and by-products which generally line the route leading towards an industrial society. The United States and Europe show similarities today not only because the United States has had a heavy impact on Europe, but because it seems that every industrial society must go through the same steps that the United States has gone through. Criticism of this Americanization process is, therefore, no more than an existential anxiety and a fear of industrial society in general.

Yet we must not overlook the fact that German-American relations have always run the risk of turning into a one-way flow from the United States to Germany alone. We remain affected by socio-political dynamics and change in the United States. The speed with which they reach us has increased considerably: It is no longer the speed of the Gulf Stream but has, for some time now, been the breathtaking speed of the jumbo jets.

The really novel element in our relationship with the United States in this decade is that we are now also importing the problems and crises of the American society. Youth protests against the supposed and actual failings of industrial society have hit us just as hard as they have hit America and just as hard as the American trade and currency crises have hit us. Even if student protest has taken different forms in Europe and West Germany, its basic character was imported from the United States by German exchange students. Other crises of modern society originating in the United States have reached West Germany. After having heard of smog in Chicago, we Germans were taken aback to find that similar environmental pollution existed in Frankfurt. The drug wave has reached us, too, as well as the wave of violence which has inundated the United States. It has become clear through the protest and even the hippie movements which seem to appeal to our young people that our youth culture is basically influenced by that of America. The "Jesus movement" is spilling over to West Germany and nostalgia is in vogue.

Our ties with the United States, thus, go beyond the dimensions of foreign policy. Our past, our present, and our future as well, have in many respects been influenced by the United States. We have to face up to the fact that the so-called "American challenge" is not just economic and political, as Servan-Schreiber warned, but infects every aspect of our life. That is why we must call upon our own capacity to use our own ideas and to develop our own intellectual creativity.

There have been times when one has wanted to give a stronger political expression to this social tie with the United States. The concept of an "Atlantic Community" was developed to characterize these comprehensive relations. On November 29, 1965, Barzel supported this idea in the German Parliament. And indeed, during the Johnson-Erhard era, it seemed for a short while as if this approach would determine the future relationship between Europe and America. But the Kiesinger administration referred again to the Atlantic Alliance in conceding that the United States has interests beyond Atlantic affairs alone, that it is involved in the full scope of world politics.

The German-American relationship has been Europeanized. For Great Britain, "the alternative to joining the European Community is to become the 51st state of the United States." This thought, expressed by the former Labour Party minister, Lord George Brown, applies to West Germany as well. In addition to its political mooring in its alliance with the United States, West Germany has tried to anchor itself to the European idea. Only he who remembers the Adenauer era correctly knows that the concept of a unified Europe initially had more attraction for the first chancellor of West Germany than Germany's relationship with the United States. The very first policy statement of the new government of West Germany aspired to overcome the hostilities in Western Europe and establish a European community. In the same statement, the United States merely received thanks for its economic and humanitarian assistance. In the face of the world political threat, the German-American alliance was born on the spur of the moment. The realization of the European concept has been largely delayed on the political agenda.

A factor in the politics of European integration is the hope of greater equality in the alliance with the United States. Bonn and the governments of the other Western European countries hope to unify in order to form a partner of equal weight to the United States which none of them could become on its own. Only a united Europe promises such a counterweight to the United States. The Americans have made it clear that they would be pleased with such a development.

Alliance issues in the seventies will clearly be approved in more of a multilateral European context than in a bilateral context. But the relations of West Germany with the United States will remain an irreplaceable condition of national security far more for us than for the other Western European countries. Questions of disarmament, détente, and American troop withdrawal from Europe are of most immediate concern to the security of West Germany even though these considerations remain significant for the other states as well. The Germans would be the first victims of any Soviet adventure that might be precipitated by a misperception on the part of the Soviets of the American willingness to fight. The alliance with the United States remains our *raison d'état.* Ours is a free society, determined to maintain and even to develop further its role in current world politics. The German-American relationship has existed for almost three decades. The Viennese writer, Alfred Polgar, once said that if you just live long enough, you will get used to the prospect of dying. Instead of getting used to the idea of dying, West Germany must develop a viable German-American relationship in order to preserve the German-American alliance necessary for its political survival. The Germans are the Europeans who can least afford to say "Goodbye, America."

9

Conflict and Consensus in the Third Postwar Decade

The continued freedom of West Germany and West Berlin is proof of how successful our alliance with the United States has been. Still, we have faced many difficulties, disagreements, and even crises. The Americans have not always understood our position. At times we have failed to understand theirs. As is natural in such an alliance, disturbances in the German-American relationship have to a large extent originated with the senior partner, the United States. For one thing, domestic politics in the United States seem particularly unpredictable. For example, strong-minded senators, who are used to seeing presidents come and go, often play a more influential role in the making of American foreign policy than the allies of the United States appreciate.

Even though President Nixon continues to be successful in gaining approval for the maintenance of the American commitment in Europe, the thought that German security depends on uncertainties which could develop as a result of American domestic politics remains a disconcerting one. As a result of developments in Congress, since the beginning of the seventies, a kind of sword of Damocles—symbolic of the prospect of a

Congressional decision on a drastic reduction of troops in Europe—has hung over the German-American relationship. Such a move would put considerable strain on the alliance. But the alliance has been strained even more by its own members' divergent evaluations of the common foe, the Soviet Union, and the differing conclusions that have resulted with regard to the world political situation. Honesty obliges an admission of the fact that the Americans perceived certain trends in Soviet moves earlier and more accurately than we. At the same time, some of the conclusions from their analyses were reached abruptly and, from the point of view of their allies, incomprehensibly, and often without the necessary consultation.

These situations have given rise time and again to policy inconsistencies which have been mainly the fault of the United States. The tempo in the development of Brandt's *Ostpolitik* provides the first instance in which West Germany has aroused anything along the lines of surprise among the Americans. It is true that American officials repeatedly said "yes" to questions concerning the United States government's attitude regarding *Ostpolitik*. Yet one can learn, without difficulty, in conversations with representatives of the Nixon administration as well as foreign policy-watchers in the United States, that they are concerned that the compromises in the German foreign policy efforts at détente might go too far.

For German-American relations in the fifties, in the sixties, and probably in the seventies as well, the basic question has been and will continue to be: How shall we deal with the Russians? At the end of the forties and in the first years of the fifties, German-American cooperation was built on a foundation of common opposition to the Soviet Union. The Berlin blockade began early in 1948. This was the first of many provocative Soviet challenges to the freedom of West Berlin. The experiences shared by Germans and Americans in the course of the airlift formed a psychological basis for German-American relations. As both countries stood side by side in repulsing the Soviet threat, they shared a crisis that tested the alliance as it has never again been so tested.

In the middle fifties, West Germany made a contribution to rearmament of the West itself and thus became an important partner of the United States in Europe. The basis for close cooperation was laid by Acheson and Dulles for the Americans and by Adenauer for the Germans. Dulles's relationship with Adenauer became almost legendary. Two politicians, made of the same stuff, seemed to have sought and found each other, tied together, above all, by their unshakable anti-Communism.

Changes in international politics have had particularly strong effects on the security strategies of the Western alliance. This development has provided a growing source of conflict between West Germany and the United States. Even during the time of maximum mutual understanding, the first warning shot was fired over the course of Western military strategy. Discussion on this issue livened up in the second half of the fifties. It was primarily a question of American control over military planning for Germany specifically, and for NATO in general. At the same time, Admiral Radford's policy of massive response stirred up considerable uneasiness in German political circles.

Discussion of the Radford Plan was soon superseded as a more complicated set of considerations came to influence NATO strategy. The Soviet Union had achieved nuclear strength equal to that of the United States. This development startled the Germans anew. Strategy discussions showed who was calling the shots and who, on the other hand, had to accept them. The United States changed strategies of its own accord, and West Germany was obliged to lend its support. It was not involved in the creation of the new NATO strategy. In fact, like all of the other NATO states, it could only contribute to the modification of details.

Around this time, West Germany first noticed changes in another realm as well. Faced with Khrushchev's Berlin ultimatum in 1958, Dulles had tried to defuse the situation by offering the Soviets a more flexible American position. As Kennedy replaced Eisenhower, more problems developed. The idol of the young people in Germany and in many other countries, Kennedy experienced a triumphant trip through West Germany and a memorable welcome in Berlin. His personality fascinated the Western world and gave it new hope. But his contribution to foreign policy questions distressed his German partners. Kennedy saw the Soviet Union as a would-be negotiating partner. Secretary of Defense Robert McNamara busied himself with a new restructuring of NATO policy. Finally, when the Berlin Wall was built, Germans had to recognize the fact that their alliance with the United States could maintain the status quo but could not change it.

As Gerhard Schröder, Foreign Minister under Adenauer and Erhard, put it, "During the sixties, the wind blew mightily through the German house." Americans and Germans struggled with each other over delicate issues on several occasions. German distrust of

America as an ally led to a flirtation with Gaullism, although it was not realized in Germany that de Gaulle could speak from a position of safety that the Germans lacked. Adenauer's great achievement of German-French reconciliation had a trace of an anti-American accent, but the Bundestag saw to it that this was toned down in the preamble which it added during the ratification of the German-French treaty.

American determination to pursue negotiations with the Soviet Union in the direction of détente grew even stronger after the Cuban missile crisis of 1962. The world had been to the brink of nuclear war. Détente thus became the decisive guideline in the international context for an approach to the German question. Through one move after another, the Germans were shown by their American partners that the theme of the fifties—first reunification and then détente—was being modified and in fact reversed. Détente would only be feasible through parallel progress in the politics of the German question. Finally, the United States made the bitter facts of the situation clear: The German question could only be solved after a successful relaxation of tensions.

These developments were accompanied by considerable strains in the alliance. As far back as Adenauer and Kennedy, the German press as well as the press around the world had portrayed the mood between the two alliance partners as having reached an unprecedented low point. It was a significant contribution of Foreign Minister Schröder, on the basis of his insight into the changing international conditions and the American point of view, that he was able to steer German foreign policy on a course which helped avoid catastrophic collisions.

In light of the nuclear stalemate, the effectiveness

of a deterrence strategy was questionable. A switch from a policy of active deterrence to one of passive deterrence was evident. Second strike capability came to be seen as decisive, and it became the new definition of a world power. At the same time, however, it raised doubts about the reliability of a nuclear guarantee. Thus, Great Britain and France came to the conclusion that they needed their own nuclear arsenals. In the case of West Germany and the other NATO countries, these states believed they needed to have a "say" on nuclear strategy. In both cases, the catalyst was European distrust of the American nuclear guarantee. The point is that, on either side of the Atlantic, there was a different view of NATO. The United States expected confidence from its partners in its guarantee, which it believed provided complete security. European arguments to the contrary were provided particularly by France along with a fair number of German Gaullists. French General Pierre Gallois expressed a skeptical point of view: "How likely is it that an alliance partner will still be defended when a nuclear trade-off between the attacker and the protecting power means suicide for both?"

As an expression of deep distrust of the United States, Gaullism was only a temporary development in the Federal Republic. A fair question is whether it might experience a renaissance in the seventies as German Gaullism à la Willy Brandt. Time will tell. During the sixties, West Germany and other European countries attempted to gain greater influence over nuclear strategy planning in NATO. In accepting the Athens Resolution of 1962, the United States promised to tie the use of atomic weapons to a system of consultation within the alliance. But there is an important qualification to the resolution: Consultation can naturally only occur to the extent that time and opportunity are available under emergency conditions. The practical question that runs through all discussions of nuclear strategy is whether one can manage without centralized control over the use of atomic weapons. This is truly a difficult problem to deal with. It has always been pointed to by the Americans as an important argument in favor of their ultimate control over the use of nuclear weapons in the field. Still, a planning group was set up to facilitate the openness of the alliance's nuclear strategy to new ideas. West Germany is a standing member.

Another German-American misunderstanding was generated by an American attempt to achieve more influence for West Germany and the other European partners. Under both Kennedy and Johnson, the Americans supported the idea of a multilateral force (MLF) in whose deployment all NATO partners were to be involved. In the course of discussing this idea, it became clear that the Germans were the members of the alliance who were most interested. Their enthusiasm led to an ever-increasing sense of isolation from the other European NATO members. Finally, they appeared to have been misled when Johnson quietly dropped the project in 1964. What the Americans had conceived of as a source of relief to German and European concerns over nuclear strategy became in the end only further ground for discord.

Is nuclear responsibility unshareable? This problem continues to worry the alliance.

When the Nuclear Test Ban Treaty was signed in August, 1963, Germany's signing was highly controversial. This was because the GDR was already a signatory, but especially because West Germans were questioning the Western alliance more and more about the extent to which it assured their security. Once again, it was only through the efforts of Schröder that West Germany was kept loyal to the alliance. In every move the Americans made, the Germans were seeing grounds for distrust. The lobby representing German concerns in Washington became a thriving concern.

In 1968, the United States and the Soviet Union signed the Non-Proliferation Treaty. From the very beginning, the Americans asked for and expected support for the treaty from West Germany. Once again there followed a fairly heated discussion between the leading power and the alliance partners. And, once again, West Germany played a central role. Some of the misunderstandings were cleared up at the diplomatic level. But the fear remained that the Americans and the Russians wanted to establish a new order of nuclear hegemony on the basis of the treaty. In this case, the German-American relationship was not the only one involved. All allies of the United States around the world were affected, especially Japan. In this case again, however, the final decision was in favor of support for the treaty. With this move, the threshold of the seventies was crossed, and *Ostpolitik* became the new theme of German-American discussion. The readiness of the Brandt government to sign the Non-Proliferation Treaty can surely be seen in connection with its wish for maximum leeway in the negotiation of *Ostpolitik*. All indications suggest that this orientation was acceptable to officials in the United States.

In 1969, the German-American alliance was confronted once again with the basic question: How shall we deal with the Soviet Union? In the negotiations leading to the Berlin agreement, the Americans found the old situation reversed. Much to the surprise of the Americans, it was West Germany that was pushing for rapid results and was ready to make compromises in German aims. But this did not get at the main question that bothered the Americans. Many officials in Washington shrugged their shoulders: "We cannot be more German than the Germans." What they actually meant was that they could not be more German than this particular German government.

But even if the Americans consider this phase of German *Ostpolitik* as only a kind of prelude to future undertakings, German and American politicians will still have to discuss the question of European security more seriously. It will be important to strengthen all of the new ties that have developed in the course of the alliance to bring each other's understanding of the situation up to date. For, if one looks at the end product of the relations between West Germany and the United States, one must admit that in the last decade our alliance has been characterized by a declining vigor. In the sixties, there was less consensus than in the fifties. Will there be even less in the seventies?

Under an excess burden in world politics, Americans widely believe that their task in Europe has been more or less accomplished. But this cannot be said with regard to the security of West Germany.

Similarly, we Germans must be careful not to conclude on the basis of the temporary overburdening of the United States that we should pursue *Ostpolitik* as far as possible on our own steam. If the Americans are to continue to provide us with protection from a possible threat from the East, we must wage our *Ostpolitik* in cooperation with them. The Soviet Union, as the object of the German *Ostpolitik* and the German-American alliance, will only take efforts at détente politics seriously if its aspirations to gain possession of America's sphere of influence are ruled out as clearly in the seventies as they have been in the past.

10

Anti-Americanism in West Germany

European anti-Americanism is as old as America itself. Ernst Fraenkel, a German political scientist, has said:

> Out of a unique mixture of an arrogant feeling of intellectual superiority compared to the "land without culture" and an almost despondent sense of economic inferiority compared to the "land of unlimited opportunities," there has resulted a distorted picture of the United States, which burdens the thinking of the old cultural states of Western Europe—and not least of all Germany—like a kind of spiritual mortgage.

There has always been the image of the wealthy American, the ultimate symbol of the affluent citizen of the Western world. During the postwar period, it was this image above all that made a distinct impression on the Germans, who saw Americans as bigger than life because of their own immediate destitution. A German scholar who returned from a stay in the United States in 1920 has described with wonder how he was surrounded by relatives and colleagues at his university.

Some asked discreetly, but other were unabashed in demanding a loan. All simply assumed that he had made money in America. "The rich uncle from America" has always haunted the German fantasies in this respect.

Since the Weimar Republic, interest in the United States has been concentrated on the technical and economic areas. The German recovery after 1950 was characterized by its attempt to model itself after the ideal provided by the United States. This approach did undergo substantial changes as experience was gained in the difficulties of running a welfare state.

There have been various instigators of anti-Americanism. What was once to be heard from the right—attacking a cultureless and much too powerful America—is now articulated from the left. The apparently indestructible, long-term feature of all criticism remains a cultural prejudice. Poet and critic Heinrich Heine's description of America as "a great stable of freedom inhabited by the boors of equality" has found a more contemporary parallel in the observation of Friedrich Dürrenmatt: "In Russia, the people are rendered stupid by the party; in the United States, by television." The Swiss playwright seems willfully to ignore the contribution of American television to an open discussion of domestic and foreign problems unknown in any other society of the world.

It is believed that the Americans, as a result of their fall from grace in Vietnam, can no longer claim to be the leading moral example in world politics.

It is true that this American claim has affected the Germans decisively on three occasions. Twice it led the United States to become Germany's opponent in war. The consequences of the third occasion, when America decided to help rebuild Germany out of the postwar chaos, are far too easily forgotten. But these antagonisms of right-wing derivation have less and less to do with the image of America that contemporary left-wing anti-Americanism is attempting to create. American controversy over the right course for the country has provided much of the fuel for European anti-Americanism. Americans on trips to Europe have felt more and more as if they've never left home as they have discovered Europeans using American arguments to make a point which is anti-American. Senator Jacob Javits, a leading thinker on American policy towards Europe, concluded that the European view of America was reminiscent of the fading image of the Ottoman Empire before World War I: "The sick man of the Bosporus" has become "the sick man on the other side of the Atlantic."

The fashionableness of anti-Americanism is even reflected in current film making styles, by both Americans and others. When everything American was extolled back in the fifties, the American superworld was portrayed in European movies in shining colors. Many of today's major films seem only to see the decline of American society; and both American and European directors are scratching beneath the surface of the gleaming American image.

One must take a look at three groups in any discussion of anti-Americanism in West Germany. One can feel a certain sympathy towards the first group. These are the young people who see war as an anachronism in our time and who have particularly high expectations for those countries in the world in whose political systems freedom and dignity have already been substantially achieved. Their standard for judging the Western democracies is more demanding than the one they apply to revolutionary Communists involved in wars of national liberation. For these young people, the war in Vietnam was an introduction to contemporary international politics and they saw the conflict only in terms of the United States as a superpower using blatant force against a mini-state. Unfortunately, they tend to see events as either all black or all white, and they tend to ignore some of the basic developments in the international politics of the last twenty to thirty years. We must maintain an intensive dialogue with these young people to keep them from falling victim to political naiveté.

With the withdrawal of the Americans, it will become clear whether the Communists follow a policy of compromise for the peaceful development of the country or whether they establish a dictatorship resulting in the imprisonment or even death of dissidents. Our politicians should make it a point to involve themselves in discussions with these young people and confront them with the potential meanings and implications of their actions as they are articulated in protests and demonstrations.

Then there is a second group that has pursued anti-Americanism on the basis of political motives. Certain Social Democratic parliamentarians, local politicians, and members of the academic community have publicly expressed anti-American attitudes. They believe a general repudiation of the German-American alliance is slowly but surely underway. Their motive? Apparently they think that anti-Americanism will force *Ostpolitik* further down the line towards the success they see for it. But personal motives play a role as well. These people want to show themselves to be the leading protagonists of the New Left. They are not concerned with any resulting foreign policy problems. Serious consideration of this development is merited by the fact that a number of these persons are party friends of Chancellor Brandt. A situation in which the Chancellor manages to create a delicate set of diplomatic porcelain in his foreign policy kiln which members of his party then smash publicly in the streets of West Germany cannot last for long. One expects more of an intellectual effort from these people when they address themselves to problems relating to the United States, particularly since they are members of the ruling political party. And again, from a political point of view, one expects even in the context of moral questions that these people should stop short of cooperation with the German Communists.

Then we come to the third group. These are the people who have developed anti-Americanism into an art. They are the "new lefters," to whom "a Red Vietnam means a free Vietnam." They thoughtlessly gave their support to the cause of the Communists in Vietnam. The moral protests of many young people in Germany are only a means to an end in which peaceful methods have no place anyhow. For example, the Young Socialist youth group of the SPD has suggested that West Germany discontinue its subsidy payments to support American troops in Europe. They have even called for the withdrawal of American troops from Europe and may finally demand that Europe cut its ties to the United States completely. These are not policies in the interests of West Germany. Whoever gives the Soviet Union reason to believe Western solidarity is crumbling spoils the future chances for the détente politics accomplished thus far. One of the domestic problems of West Germany resulting from *Ostpolitik* is that Chancellor Brandt, as chairman of the SPD, has found it more difficult to get his point across to the Young Socialists. Anti-Americanism has become the subject of concern even in the rivalries within West Germany's strongest party, the SPD.

Two tendencies must be watched very carefully if the anti-American wave is not to become a political issue endangering the political systems of Europe and West Germany. The first tendency is particularly obvious. Criticism of the United States aims, in fact, at all social systems in the Western world. It affects the German-American relationship both at its base and in its long-term perspective.

But the second tendency is even more real and more dangerous. A political climate that fosters popular support of American withdrawal from Europe is growing as a result of the broadening scope of anti-Americanism. An effort is being made to show the United States and the Soviet Union to be moral equivalents. According to this point of view, both the United States and the Soviet Union are world powers which want only to establish hegemony over Europe. They both resort to the same methods. Neither society is acceptable as a model for Europe. NATO is seen as the equivalent of the Warsaw Pact, and the developments in Czechoslovakia are compared to those in Vietnam. In his *Sentences from America,* Friedrich Dürrenmatt has written: "The main difference between Russia and America today is that in Russia everyone presumes he is a gangster." Another parallel was suggested by a leading SPD politician. In his opinion, Soviet troops in Czechoslovakia were no different from the American troops in Germany. The sad fact is that the differences between a free way of life, on the one hand, and a dictatorship, on the other, are never taken into account in these comparisons.

But this view comes up again and again in conversations with people in West Germany. Many young people especially do not realize that this perspective distorts the actual situation of people in both systems in practical as well as theoretical terms. Under more intense questioning, they will even concede that the East comes out of their analysis looking better than the West. Their final line of argument is that a view like this is a logical outgrowth of the current atmosphere of détente, particularly after twenty years of anti-Communist propaganda.

The same ominous mistake has been made in a number of political commentaries written in West Germany. To give more drive to the new *Ostpolitik*, to support it firmly, and to render the Russians more acceptable as negotiating partners for peace agreements in Europe, the attempt is made to create as much sympathy as possible for the problems of the Communist system and to emphasize ongoing achievements, with a totally unskeptical attitude.

What about understanding and tolerance for the problems of the United States? Many have yet to realize that the stirring up of American waters is most likely to provide more power for the Soviet mills to grind out a policy of gaining influence over Europe. The distrust of the United States as an alliance partner that has been shown in some aspects of official policy might fuse with the elements of anti-American feeling manifest in current public opinion and become a motive behind a stimulated German *Ostpolitik*. Were this to occur, the one-sidedness and the distortion of the contemporary image of the United States could become a political issue of the first order. Instead of providing for the penetration of barriers, under such conditions, *Ostpolitik* would generate a new dimension of ideological tension.

Among broad segments of our population an awareness of the vital necessity for our alliance with the United States remains as clear as ever. The insight of these persons into the problems facing the United States has increased, too. At the same time, there is a growing uncertainty over the need for American troops in Germany. Recently, a public opinion poll showed that only one-third of the population ruled out all possibility of maintaining the country's security if the American troops were to be withdrawn. The most current polls even show a trend towards favoring neutrality for West Germany. In 1971, half of those asked supported German neutrality along the lines of the Swiss example.

The German-American relationship should not be allowed to become a topic that is too sensitive to be discussed. It should be German policy to stimulate basic discussion of the question in all of its ramifications and especially with regard to the interest of today's youth. We should not stand silent in the face of the new anti-Americanism. In such organizations as the American Council on Germany in the United States and the Atlantic Bridge in Germany, leading figures from all fields have a regular opportunity for an ongoing German-American exchange of ideas. But the concern that has grown for the German-American alliance because of these expressions of anti-Americanism should not be limited to these groups alone. Official policy discussion between government and parties must be built on a realistic view of the United States. The weaknesses, the strengths, and the trend of developments in American society must be taken into consideration in the planning of the future of the Western democracies and their industrial societies.

11

The Politics of Détente in Europe

If the West is not prepared for both détente and tension in the world politics of the 1970s, it is the Soviet Union then that will determine the rhythm and content of the coming politics of détente. This could easily lead to an expansion of Soviet hegemony in Europe. To prevent this from happening, the West must come up with initiatives of its own or the result of détente will be more security for the Soviet Union and less for us.

In the years following Stalin's death in 1953, the world discussed the prospects of détente. At that time reference was made to the spirit of the Geneva talks of 1955 and later to the spirit of the Camp David meeting of 1959. The Soviets spoke of "peaceful coexistence." New prospects for détente between the Soviet Union and the United States were taking shape. But then the Cuban missile crisis of 1962 brought this possibility to an abrupt halt. Kennedy's "strategy for peace" offered a new approach to the situation, and shortly contacts between East and West began again. President Johnson maintained readiness for negotiations, and finally in 1967, NATO published the Harmel Report in which it listed détente as well as defense as its two main tasks.

The policy of détente was described in a supplementary note added to the final communiqué of the NATO ministers conference in December 1967:

> The Atlantic Alliance has two main functions. The first includes the maintenance of sufficient military strength and political solidarity to provide a deterrent against aggression and other forms of pressure and a defense of the territories of member states in the case of aggression. The second function of NATO includes a continuing search for progress towards lasting relations that will contribute to the solution of basic political questions. Military security and a policy of détente are not contradictory concepts. Instead, they supplement each other mutually.

Attempts to improve East-West relations in Europe have been a continuing theme of the NATO conferences. In Brussels, in December 1970, the Alliance articulated principles which were to provide guidelines for "exploratory talks": "Equal status based on the sovereignty, political independence, and territorial integrity of each European state; noninterference with the domestic affairs of any state, regardless of its political or social system; and the right of the people of each European state to determine its own fate, free from external pressures."

The United States and West Germany will have key roles to play in the coming efforts at an improvement of East-West relations in Europe. Both are concerned with their future in Europe, and any détente proposal will have an effect on their positions. For the United States, it is a question of maintaining its leadership role in the Western alliance, especially in the context of

European affairs. For West Germany, it is, above all, a question of its continuing membership in the Western alliance. Proposals of the Soviet Union have a two-pronged objective—simultaneous attempts to push the United States out of its European involvement and to lure West Germany away from the Western alliance.

For the time being, the American umbrella of protection remains indispensable while West Germany and the other West European countries attempt to achieve European unification. This goal must be reached during the coming decade. When the Soviet Union proposes a European security system, it is clearly thinking of a peace on Soviet terms. Implied in this are the classic goals of its European policy: withdrawal of the United States from Europe and the extension of Soviet hegemony over all of the Continent. This danger will be all the more real if the Soviet Union and the United States agree formally to be the joint guarantors of such an "all-European security system." This would allow for a substantial reduction of existing American commitments in Europe. As a consequence, a new orientation or even a race among Western European countries for an arrangement with the Soviet Union might easily result.

There can be no doubt that given such a configuration of European politics, even the domestic order of West Germany would not remain untouched by Communist influence. Western Europeans cannot give their political blessing to the Soviet oppression of Eastern Europe. A change in policy would not only contradict the principles for the pursuit of détente articulated by NATO in December 1970, but in the long run would contradict the very concept of European détente itself.

As long as peace in the sense conceived of by Soviet

ideologists means Communist class struggle and does not include a readiness to accept the Western political and social order, Europe must continue to differentiate between a Soviet and American peace. For the present, there is no substitute for a peace on American terms which guarantees the freedom of the Western European states. Only future agreements between East and West and a firm Soviet commitment to a policy of noninterference in the domestic affairs of Western European states could lead to a revision of this judgment. Only then would we see a real beginning of détente in Europe. West Germany has made a beginning with its *Ostopolitik*. These efforts have essentially been aimed in the right direction in their attempt to gain concrete results for Berlin and the people of a divided Germany.

Western Détente Policy

Western détente policy has basically been tied to three very concrete hopes: first, that the partition of Europe will be made more tolerable by cultural and human contacts of all kinds; second, that with the reduction of tensions, funds now spent for defense will be saved; and third, that trade with the East will promote the expansion of the Western economy. These hopes provide many incentives for concrete agreements, and they are supported by a steadily growing feeling of security among the European peoples in East and West. The West is ready for détente. The strongly diminished fear of armed conflict on the Continent certainly provides a psychological underpinning for the efforts for détente.

There are many international political factors relevant to the prospects for détente on the European continent. One is that Europe has become less important as a place in which conflicts may occur. The spotlight is now on other parts of the world. In the future, the two superpowers, the United States and the Soviet Union, will have so many conflicts in Asia and elsewhere to deal with that they will welcome détente on the European scene. We only have to look at the war between India and Pakistan and its international implications for the Soviet Union, the United States, and China, to see an example of the shift of focus from Europe to elsewhere.

A broad basis of hope for détente in Europe, finally, is seen in the parallel directions of the industrial societies of both East and West. According to this view, Western and Communist societies must strain to raise the rates of economic growth to meet consumer demands in such a way that they will both be using roughly similar methods. A likely result will be a similarity in living conditions and attitudes, and this, in turn, could lead to a lessening of the contrasts between opposing ideologies. A convergence of the two systems, spurred on by factors inherent in industrialization, could also be accelerated by an acceptance of the responsibility common to all of the developed countries of Europe to provide foreign aid to the Third World.

This panorama of hopes for détente can only be tested and brought closer to reality through political action. To pursue a policy of détente in this sense calls for careful preparation. One cannot proceed merely by wishful thinking. West Germany must be ready for both cooperation and confrontation in the seventies. Our intention to cooperate with the East will find its limits at that point at which we are threatened with giving up our freedom and forgoing our alliance with the West.

This is the most important lesson to be learned from the Bonn *Ostpolitik:* It has evoked a determined will for peace in the West, but still not convincingly in the East. But our determination for peace should not be mistaken in future negotiations for a willingness to make unlimited concessions. Détente policy and Western readiness for conciliation can reach a point at which they lead to new tensions. Western concessions can induce the East to become aggressive or exert pressure. That is the lesson we must learn from the appeasement policy leading to the Second World War. In the case of the détente policy of the NATO powers, we should be well aware of the self-assuredness demonstrated by Soviet reliance on military power as a factor in international negotiations. The more uncertain the Western willingness to fight back becomes, the more uncertain become the hopes for peace in Europe. The military threat presented by the Soviet Union cannot be dismissed. CFurthermore, the revival of such old concepts as "disengagement," "denuclearized zone," and "limited disarmament in Central Europe," which originated at a time of aggressive Soviet foreign policy, should not induce the Western alliance to diminish its defense preparedness. As a German commentator remarked: "When there is no longer fear of an enemy, the alliance ends; only then can it make that contribution to détente."

The paradox of the European balance of power renders peace defensible only through continuous Western efforts to promote defense preparedness. NATO must remain a convincing organ of both nuclear and conventional military might. Countess Marion Dönhoff, political commentator and winner of the German Publishers' Peace Prize of 1970, described in her acceptance speech the policy with which Western Europeans should pursue future negotiations in search of détente:

> I think we have reached the end of a sterile epoch and have come to the beginning of a new chapter, the Outline of Peace. This would refer to a phase in which one problem is carefully approached after another, shared interests are developed and conflicts defused, while the unsolvable questions are tabled for the moment. Such a process will demand a great deal of patience and a great deal of hair-splitting. Advocates of major change will not be satisfied. In short, it will not be an heroic epoch, but a period of wearying detail-work. But it is worth giving it a try.

The Will for Détente in the Soviet Union

Whoever considers the topic of *Ostpolitik* will also speculate about the intentions of the Soviet Union. Henry Kissinger has remarked: "The dispute on the intentions of the Communists has diverted our attention from an elaboration of our own position. In some circles the question of whether Soviet intentions have been given the benefit of the doubt is regarded as the acid test for an active position in favor of peace."

"The problems involved in the transition of the United States from the industrial to the post-industrial era have been similar to challenges faced by the Soviet Union in the growing dysfunction of its political system in terms of societal progress and economic growth." This view of the American expert on Soviet affairs, Zbigniew Brzezinski, on Soviet domestic immobility is the theme of similar analyses that have been made in the

West. Since the Soviet Union needs technological know-how and methods of modern management from the West in order to achieve social and economic progress, its leadership must be active in international politics. Compared with the Common Market, the Soviet Union is equal in population size but lags in all sectors of production. An additional indication of its economic inferiority to the Common Market is the state of development of its computer technology. The Soviet Union entered the seventies with the same number of computers as that of West Germany alone. The economic and cultural lag of the Soviet Union creates a decisive political problem for that country of how to distribute its investment funds between heavy and light industry. In other words, the challenge involves the question of guns or butter—determining the proportion of armaments versus consumer goods. Therefore, many in the West expect that growth of the Soviet industrial society will lead to a convergence of sorts with that of the West.

But can this convergence in the economic and technological sphere proceed parallel with a degeneration in Soviet domestic politics described by German journalist, Wolfgang Leonhard, as "limited neo-Stalinism"? It is seen in a tightening-up of controls in the cultural sphere, heightened censorship in the mass media, and new restrictions on Soviet intellectuals. The infamous asylums which provide a new method to quiet dissidents are another aspect of this trend. But there are other features of the conservative neo-Stalinist character of the Brezhnev regime. The armaments budget of the Soviet Union is still rising drastically. There are educational campaigns of a militarist nature. Brezhnev has called for ideological struggle against "right-wing opportunists," "Trotskyites," "revisionists," and other "dissidents." There has been an increase in domestic opposition to these new controls, but it is quite powerless against the state campaign of indoctrination.

The isolated and cohesive élite of the Soviet Union is an obstacle to the completion of the country's development as a modern industrial society. Such an élite gives the Soviet Union many characteristics reminiscent of the late-Victorian era. The country's national hubris is shown in its current wish to establish an international Pax Sovietica dictated from Moscow, which is supported by the fact that travel to foreign countries is still restricted even for leading politicians. The seclusive life style of the leading stratum with its own shopping facilities and residence quarters still contributes to the prevention of close contact between the élite and the masses in the Soviet Union. And doesn't the determination shown by the Soviet Union in building up its naval fleet at exorbitant costs in order to show its colors all over the world betray most clearly these traits of late-Victorian hubris?

All power in politics, economics, science, culture and information is still centrally located within the Party oligarchy. This is the same group that has been so clumsy in effecting change in the industrial sector and of which one cannot say with certainty whether it has given up the Soviet claim to world domination. At least there is no evidence in the Soviet Union as of now of the weariness with which the United States seems to view its role as a world power. Furthermore, the role of a world power can no longer be seen as only ideologically motivated. The current situation of world Communism has shown the Soviet Union that it is no longer the sole ruling center of a world Communist movement. The Soviet Union has had to recognize a decay of its authority in the international sphere. It can no longer even realistically hope for parallel progress in both world revolution and Soviet expansion. Those times are definitely gone, because not every revolution, not even every Communist revolution in the world, represents an event advantageous for the Soviet Union. In certain respects, the Chinese have spoiled Soviet efforts in foreign affairs. Nevertheless, it is clear that because the export of Communism is no longer only in the immediate self-interest of the Soviet Union and that not every case of conversion to Communism is to its natural advantage alone, the foreign policy of Soviet Russia has more and more become that of a big power increasingly concerned with its own national interests.

In looking at the Soviet Union, we have to deal with some contradictions. In spite of the advanced age of Soviet top leadership—Brezhnev, Kosygin, Podgorny and Suslov are all approaching their seventies—Soviet foreign policy has become unusually flexible. Look at the developments in India, in the Middle East, in Latin America. Think of the travel-cum-diplomacy on the part of the Soviet leaders. And last but not least, look at the Soviet response to the Bonn *Ostpolitik* and the Soviet diplomatic offensive in Western Europe.

At the annual convention of the Society for East European Studies, Richard Löwenthal, the German political scientist and leading scholar of international Communism, saw as a counterpart to the Party's maintenance of power in domestic affairs, the priority given to the consolidation of the Soviet international position in foreign policy. Is this to say the Soviet Union is a status quo power?

As early as 1965, Adenauer shocked the delegates of the CDU Federal Party convention with his statement that the Soviet Union had to be counted among the peace-loving nations. In his own way of expressing trends succinctly, Adenauer was saying that the foreign policy of the Soviet Union included among its objectives not only expansive but also defensive goals, *i.e.*, the defense of its status quo position. So which is the Soviet Union: a power pressing towards Western Europe or a power which merely wants to consolidate its hegemony over Eastern Europe? Does it want to isolate West Germany from its Western partners or does it sincerely want to cooperate with West Germany as a Western industrial power in the economic and technical sphere? Is the European Security Conference supposed to bring a recognition of the existing relationships or the beginning of the dissolution of the Western alliance? The West is well advised not to search for an answer to these questions by trying to analyze Soviet intentions, but rather to develop its own positive policy. If the West begins to negotiate with the Soviet Union, without giving up its efforts geared towards European unification and the improvement of the NATO defense, the Soviet Union will learn quickly enough that détente politics are no longer the means by which it can harass the West but only a means by which a reduction of tensions in Europe can be achieved. The intentions of the Soviet Union will become clearer when the intentions of the West become clearer.

The New Ostpolitik: *Wanderlust* and *Weltanschauung?*

One can be sure that there are special reasons for it when Anglo-Saxons accept German words in their vocabulary. *Ostpolitik* is such a word. Although for years the Americans pressured us to undertake our own efforts for détente with the East, they still find the current policies of the Brandt administration very original. And so they refer to them by the German term. In the context of Germany's policy in relation to the United States during the coming years, we shall have to avoid the association of *Ostpolitik* with some other terms that the Americans have also taken over from the German: *Wanderlust* and *Weltanschauung*. *Ostpolitik* should not be misunderstood merely as a travel spree or as a new ideology, but rather as a pragmatic move complementing West Germany's Western orientation.

Are there, in fact, disagreements between West Germany and the United States on the subject of *Ostpolitik?* Not officially. After the early disapproval of some well-known veterans of American policymaking for Germany subsided, *Ostpolitik* won official support in the United States. It is broadly supported by American public opinion. *Time* magazine named Willy Brandt the "Man of the Year" in 1971 on the basis of his foreign policy and led the international wave of praise for the German *Ostpolitik*. Visits by the German Chancellor to the United States have furnished additional proof of the support of the President of the United States and the government.

The Americans have always emphasized that they see these developments as a German affair. But American diplomats and political analysts were naturally startled that the Germans so suddenly gave up the legal claims they had maintained so tenaciously for so long. Furthermore, they see the race of many Western European government officials to Moscow as evidence of distrust of the European policy of the United States. For this reason, there is a need for a new German policy towards the United States—a policy that will raise our concern for America to a level equal to that of our current concern for Europe and the East. Government statements are no longer sufficient to do the job. They have usually argued that the German-American relationship is steady, firm and unwavering, and hence a sound foundation for German policies for both Europe and the East. In fact, however, the German-American alliance has been affected by current developments in Europe to an extent that could easily precipitate substantial changes in this most important of Germany's foreign relations.

German *Ostpolitik* need not be anti-American. Not only has the government officially made this claim, but developments in *Ostpolitik* up to this point have shown it to be true. Gerhard Schröder, perhaps the most successful foreign minister West Germany has ever had, knew how to accommodate the German *Ostpolitik* to America's foreign policy without friction. This was evident in his successful efforts to strengthen German contacts with the Eastern European states, particularly in the establishment of trade missions. The same diplomatic skill was shown in the peace note issued by Chancellor Erhard when he first proposed the concept of renunciation of force to Europeans in 1966. With an attempt to stimulate inter-German talks with the GDR, the establishing of diplomatic relations with Yugoslavia and Romania, and the de facto dropping of the Hallstein Doctrine, Kiesinger's Grand Coalition government proceeded in full harmony with the Americans, who were then working with the Soviets to negotiate the Non-Proliferation Treaty. The fourth phase of German *Ostpolitik* since Adenauer's time, finally, has been pursued by Brandt.

The continuity of these efforts is immediately clear. The politics of peace have always been the number one goal of West Germany, no matter who has been Chancellor. Adenauer's priorities were ranked in the order of freedom, peace, and unity, even though official government statements in the fifties and sixties often named reunification as the country's primary aim. In 1966, the Kiesinger administration cited the need for a "just and lasting order of peace" as the first priority of German foreign policy.

Brandt's peace policies are based on the reasonable assumption that there are two ways to approach security problems. On the one hand, defense must be maintained against a potential aggressor. On the other hand, a reduction of tensions will contribute to the elimination of possible causes of conflict.

The second approach has only gradually become viable for the Germans. Those who are familiar with the basic currents of European history during the fifties and sixties will see how Germans regard this as a bitter necessity. The Soviet Union's repeated stimulation of crises in Berlin alone support this objective. The Berlin Agreement and its implementation provide a critical test for the chances of a further reduction of tensions between the East and West in Europe. Thus, the aim of securing the peace has been a continuing theme of German foreign policy.

Brandt undertook his *Ostpolitik* to achieve a relaxation of tensions in the East by making German concessions to the Soviet Union. This peacemaking move was applauded throughout the world, and won for Brandt the Nobel Peace Prize. Germany's readiness to accept sacrifices in its negotiations with the Soviet Union and other Eastern European nations has shown the extent to which West Germany is willing to bear costs to itself in its efforts to improve détente in Europe. There always remains the risk, of course, that the preliminary achievements of *Ostpolitik* might be in vain. This is particularly true in the case of the Basic Treaty between the two Germanys. The GDR might retract the concessions it made on freedom of movement at any time.

However, as clearly noted, the reaction of the international community to West Germany's new *Ostpolitik* has been generally favorable. But it is often not clearly understood why this policy encountered substantial domestic criticism in Germany. On the international level, one tends to see only the end results of *Ostpolitik* as a whole, while the methods by which this policy is applied on a day-to-day basis are a matter of far less interest. In fact, even if one is in emphatic agreement with the need for an active *Ostpolitik* in view of the demands of the international political situation, one must state that the way in which *Ostpolitik* has been pursued by Bonn up to this point has been regrettable. It has been applied too hastily and with insufficient coordination with our allies. It has been too yielding with regard to the issues. The hastiness shown by the German side to negotiate can only be explained by pressing political concerns of the SPD/FDP government at home. After the defeat of the Kiesinger government, *Ostpolitik* was chosen as the field in which the Brandt administration could quickly gain a favorable political profile in West Germany.

Thus, the tempo of *Ostpolitik* has often been a result less of international necessity than of the political needs of the government in connection with state or parliamentary elections. This was particularly the case when the Basic Treaty with the GDR was negotiated before the elections of November 1972. The GDR gained an advantage in the negotiating process since it knew that the government of West Germany wanted and needed a successful resolution of the negotiations before the parliamentary elections.

From an international point of view, it is sufficient to know that the Brandt government pursued these policies with the support of a majority of the German electorate. To understand the domestic controversy, however, one must take the domestic concerns of the government into consideration to be able to evaluate the general situation. The basic outlooks of the two parties on foreign policy are actually not very different from each other. The Christian Democratic opposition made the ratification of the Moscow and Warsaw treaties possible through its abstention at the critical parliamentary vote. This was at a time when the Brandt government had lost its majority in the parliament. The Christian Democrats also approved the predecessor of the Basic Treaty, the Traffic Agreement between West Germany and the GDR. The opposition has only refused to support the recently concluded Basic Treaty.

This Basic Treaty between the two German states was the most significant achievement in a series of negotiations within the framework of German *Ostpolitik*. The process began with the Moscow Treaty and continued with the treaty with Warsaw. In the summer of 1973 the treaty between Bonn and Prague was also negotiated. The inter-German talks on traffic from West Germany to West Berlin proceeded along parallel lines, supported by the Four-Power Agreement on Berlin. Membership for both German states in the United Nations will represent the formal conclusion of the inter-German part of *Ostpolitik*.

Ostpolitik has resulted in a confirmation of the status quo by the signers of the treaty in East and West. But anyone who wants to understand German politics in the future must realize that while this process has involved a confirmation of the status quo, it is not by any means a final peace agreement. The German question has not been resolved. It is true that the treaties concluded in the spirit of the renunciation of force have the general character of a boundary agreement. But it is clearly stated in the clauses of these treaties themselves, in the declarations of intent amended by West Germany and in the interpretive notes made public by the German parliament at the various instances of ratification, that the treaties are not recognized as providing ultimate resolution of the subjects with which they deal.

This is particularly true in the case of the Basic Treaty. The GDR insisted on its independence, its autonomy, and its delimited status. West Germany maintained its aim of national unity and the concept of a lasting tie between all Germans. The treaty built a compromise between the two points of view, based on the realities of the current situation. It also created a "special relationship" which will continue to lend the German question political weight in international politics.

That this is true has already been shown in the implementation of the Four-Power Agreement on Berlin. The leading planner of Bonn's *Ostpolitik,* as well as its outstanding negotiator, Egon Bahr, felt at the conclusion of the Berlin Agreement that from now on, as far as was "humanly foreseeable," Berlin could be considered secure. One would *hope* that Berlin will be secure in the future as a result of the Agreement, but past experience with the Communists, which should contribute substantially to an evaluation of the situation, speaks to the contrary.

In any case, one can almost be sure that the Four Power Agreement and Bonn's *Ostpolitik* will not be enough to move the Soviet Union to rule out using West Berlin as a springboard for the creation of international political tensions at some future time. It will, therefore, be a task for Western foreign policy to interpret the agreement as it stands in an aggressive fashion and also pursue insofar as possible close political cooperation between West Germany and West Berlin. Below the level of responsibilities set for the Four Powers, a particularly acute responsibility has fallen to West Germany. It must help to sustain West Berlin's ability to survive and it must help to see that the appeal of the city to both its inhabitants and visitors continues to grow. The Berlin Agreement will be meaningful only if Western policy is dedicated to the maintenance of Berlin and our ability to gain full Soviet understanding of this commitment.

Recently an American businessman remarked casually that West Germany could be occupied by the Soviet Union more easily than West Berlin because the United States considered the city its "own property." The people of Berlin would certainly be happy to hear this. They have always been the Germans most interested in German-American relations. The conclusion and implementation of the Berlin Agreement thus in a sense symbolizes the significance of the German-American alliance to West Germany.

In 1972, West Germany concluded a distinct three-year phase of its *Ostpolitik*. During this phase Germany was able to decide on its own the tempo and the substance of these diplomatic initiatives in its bilateral negotiations with the East. These were the years in which its Western allies articulated the preliminary requirements for efforts at European détente that might be pursued within the context of the MBFR talks and the European Security Conference. After the bilateral phase of its *Ostpolitik*, West Germany now must accommodate itself to the requirements of a multilateral nature. Certainly the Brandt government achieved a substantial number of the preliminary requirements for a wider détente in Europe through its innovative *Ostpolitik*. The problems related to the participation of the GDR in international European conferences no longer exists. At the same time, West Germany gained new freedom for itself in negotiations and can join the East-West efforts for European détente as a partner with equal rights.

12

New Forms of Nuclear Partnership

Both *Ostpolitik* and the planned disarmament talks will serve the interests of the Soviet Union and the United States as channels of communication in Europe. For countries like West Germany, France, and Great Britain, the big-power discussions, however, might well result in a change in the balance of power. Specifically, the risk exists that, presuming the continuity of past American guarantees of European security, concessions might be made to the Soviet Union which would compromise those guarantees. In spite of all the official statements made to the contrary by the German government, *Ostpolitik* is seen by some as a cautious attempt to put more distance between it and a weakened United States. West Germany must take care that its *Ostpolitik* does not develop into a policy that lends credence to that view. As long as the approach of the Soviet Union to the planned talks on European disarmament is geared towards the elimination of American influence on our continent or at least a considerable reduction thereof, West Germany must be careful lest military disarmament take place at the expense of its political position.

Dean Acheson once said that military might casts

a political shadow. The Germans and all of the Western Europeans must be careful that the Russian shadow grows no larger. In point of fact, Russian military might continues to grow as it has in the past. Evidence for this is available in the regular reviews published by the British Institute for Strategic Studies. There may be occasional controversy among military experts over the comparative figures, but in terms of conventional forces in Europe there is general agreement that the defense posture of the Soviet Union is superior to that of NATO and is becoming more so. Many Western politicians want to cross off their agendas the question of security as the leading consideration and make détente the number-one priority. These men see warnings concerning the growth of Soviet forces merely as instances of exaggerated alarm over what their own optimism tells them is no more than a tempest in a teapot.

Isolation of West Germany is the reverse side of the coin of Soviet interests, the front side of which pursues American disengagement from Europe. For this reason, the Germans will be those most interested in the coming negotiations on security and détente in Europe. They can only see the agreements they have made with the East being honored if there exists a credibility about Western defense preparedness. They also want to maintain their newly-won political position both inside and outside the framework of the Western security system. During the winter session of NATO at the end of 1971, West Germany revealed this aim in concrete terms. The agreement covering the costs of stationing American troops in Germany was extended for two years. West Germany also announced that it was ready to carry a larger proportion of the additional costs needed for the improvement of NATO's military structure than the other countries of Europe. The best proof the American administration can give to Congress as to whether the Europeans have understood the Nixon Doctrine is to point out the increased efforts at sharing of the defense burden among the Europeans themselves.

The Europeans have understood this. As a spokesman for the European group in NATO, British Defense Minister Lord Carrington was able to refer to the "European White Paper" in which the European countries had developed a supplementary "Billion-Dollar Program" on a collective basis. This certainly provides important support for Nixon's policies until results may be achieved in the MBFR talks. The situation relieves the Europeans of the necessity for conducting two-sided negotiations, on the one hand with America, and on the other, with the Soviet Union. All Europeans should by now be aware of the following: Were the Soviet Union to gain the impression that the West might unilaterally undertake troop reductions without demanding Russian concessions, then it would place its trust in the passage of time and not in negotiations.

The MBFR Talks: A Path into Insecurity

Let us next deal with the suggestion provided by NATO itself for "mutual and balanced force reductions," MBFR in short. At its summer session in 1968 in Réykjavik, Iceland, NATO offered the following guidelines: "Troop reductions on both sides should be mutual and balanced according to scope and timing. They should contribute to the maintenance of the current level of security at reduced costs. They should not be pursued in such a way as to allow a disadvantageous change in the condition of Europe as a result." For some time, NATO received no answer to this statement, even though it renewed its invitation to negotiations along these lines in 1970. Brezhnev finally indicated interest in the prospect in his speech at Tiflis. MBFR talks became the main subject of the NATO session that followed. Above all, there was a procedural question to be dealt with: How should negotiations between NATO and the Warsaw Pact be undertaken?

In its report on the military balance of power in the years 1971 and 1972, the Institute for Strategic Studies in London delineated the problem area with which the negotiating powers will be confronted in the anticipated MBFR talks. The numerical strength and equipment of troops are not the only factors that need to be taken into consideration. Qualitative characteristics such as geographic advantages, deployment requirements, and training and recruitment must also be discussed. One should also remember the differing political outlooks and military strategies that are confronting both sides in this case. An inevitable and enormous problem involved in all such attempts at disarmament is the current rate of new developments in weapons technology which just as speedily can always make negotiated settlements obsolete. The potential for such changes and, above all, the unalterable geographic advantages of the Warsaw Pact countries and the Soviet Union will be major subjects for discussion in the MBFR negotiations.

These reasons also make it clear that the problems involved in these negotiations can in no way be solved only within the context of military considerations. In fact, it is more likely that the negotiators in the MBFR talks will be addressing themselves more to the political aspects of détente than to the strictly military matters.

Only in an atmosphere of mutual trust between the two blocs can the negotiations lead to success. (Incidentally, this process must include Soviet acceptance of on-site inspection on its territory, a very touchy subject with Soviet negotiators.) But military agreements on disarmament will only be credible when political results within the context of détente come about. A reduction in the military sector and a reduction of tensions clearly go hand in hand.

The beginnings of European détente politics, including Germany's *Ostpolitik*, have changed nothing in the basic fact of Soviet military superiority and the continuing development of its military advantage. The Soviet Union did not demobilize its forces at the end of World War II, but used them as a hammer to nail its Eastern European satellites into place. Soviet military deployment is considerably more extensive than would be necessary merely for a defense alliance directed towards the West. Among other roles, this deployment also serves a kind of "political function" that holds the Soviet sphere of influence under control. The Soviet troops in Eastern Europe are more the overseers of the Germans, Hungarians, and Czechs and lately instruments of pressure on Rumania and Yugoslavia than they are providers of defense against a threat from the West.

The subjugation of the peoples of Eastern Europe and the Germans of the GDR, the construction of the Berlin Wall, and the total isolation of all of the Eastern states from the West are political realities that must be seen in connection with a second set of realities: the German desire for reunification, the binding tie between West Germany and West Berlin, and the desire of the countries of Eastern Europe for greater freedom and political self-determination.

The efforts to gain security on the part of the Soviet Union are basically different from those of the West. The West has no fear of Soviet ideas but is concerned about Soviet weaponry. The leading power of the East fears the ideas of the Western Europeans, but not their weapons. After centuries of bitter enmity, the Western countries have learned that they need not fear each other any more. In the Eastern bloc, however, the Soviet Union has moved militarily against its own allies on several occasions since World War II. A policy based only on the realities achieved through Soviet military might can hardly guarantee peace and security in Europe.

This police function of Soviet military power and its meaning for Russia's security interests will complicate all aspects of the MBFR talks. American troops stationed in Western Europe do not at all serve in such a capacity. The political systems of the Western European states would be just as stable without the presence of the American troops. Were American troops to be withdrawn, however, there would be a risk that the Soviet Union would be able to force the Western states, including West Germany, to make changes in their political systems. Without guidelines for the form and scope of troop reductions and political arrangements geared towards détente in Europe, the Soviet Union will remain a European power with forces deployed over a huge area through the countries of the Warsaw Pact alliance.

Even if the Soviet Union were to withdraw twice as many troops as did the West, it would still maintain its superiority. Comparisons of military statistics aside, the ultimate safeguard is the American guarantee for Europe, and only this guarantee can keep the Soviet Union from taking advantage of its superior military position in Europe. In a period of high tension, it is believed the Soviet Union could deploy an army of more than one hundred divisions in Eastern Europe within three weeks. It has almost twice as many tanks and fighter planes available through the Warsaw Pact than the Western countries do through NATO. This situation is further marked by the remarkable mobility of the Soviet forces especially compared to that of the Americans. The Russians can always be there faster than the Americans. Military experts say that the Soviets could comfortably withdraw eight of their soldiers for every American and still maintain their geographic advantage.

A major question that the MBFR negotiations will raise for the European states of the Western alliance is that of the balance of power. The efforts of these countries in the defense sphere, in addition to their diplomatic undertakings, were successful in achieving a balance of power between the East and West after World War II, but mainly on the basis of the nuclear guarantee of the United States. That promise of nuclear protection has provided the real guarantee for the maintenance of peace in Europe. The current feeling of security among Europeans is based upon it and the climate suitable for European détente politics has resulted from it.

Just how easily the MBFR talks might affect this balance of power is shown in NATO's current doctrine of flexible response. According to it, the allies of the United States should first defend themselves with conventional weapons. Only after the insufficiency of this response has been shown would the tactical nuclear weapons which the United States has stationed in Europe be put to use. The strategic nuclear arsenal of the allies is the last link in the chain of deterrence. The raison d'être of this strategy is to raise the threshold of nuclear war as high as possible. The build-up of conventional forces to meet the initial blows of warfare has been the result. The MBFR talks might render this strategy obsolete, one which, in any event, has always been questioned by the conventional powers of NATO. The Americans have replied emphatically that a "big lift" action could airlift troops from America to Europe very quickly to provide the full conventional strength necessary. Since the Warsaw Pact countries invaded Czechoslovakia, however, there have been doubts about the true potential of the "big lift" concept. In that incident, the Soviet Union moved its troops with unexpected rapidity. The American general, Lyman Lemnitzer, compared the resulting revelation of the differing mobility potentials of the Warsaw Pact and NATO in this case to that of the race between the tortoise and the hare.

The MBFR negotiations will, therefore, involve not only East-West relations but also relations among the Western states themselves. The talks will raise questions about NATO strategy and the future of conventional arms in Europe.

The European Security Conference: A United Europe?

Is it an omen for détente politics in Europe that the Western effort via MBFR has been advancing much more slowly than the European Security Conference (ESC) that was initiated on the basis of a suggestion from the East? As far back as the conference on Germany attended by the Four Powers in Berlin in February 1954, Soviet Foreign Minister Molotov called for a "conference of the European states" for the purpose of "arriving at a treaty on collective security." The anti-American aspect of the proposed project was evident in the fact that the United States and China were to participate only as observers. During the course of succeeding years, the Russians made renewed initiatives of this sort which encountered little Western support. Towards the end of the sixties, however, the Western states began to show interest in the prospects for holding such a conference. Since that time there has been much discussion of a possible conference on European security and cooperation. Actually, achievements in terms of cooperation between East and West are more likely at this conference than any improvement in the conditions of military security in Europe.

The first step of the diplomatic offensive on the part of the Soviet Union in recent times was the Bucharest Conference of the Warsaw Pact states. After the intervention in Czechoslovakia, the Soviet Union's interest in a European Security Conference was reiterated in Budapest in 1969. For the first time, however, in their call for a Conference, the Warsaw Pact states addressed themselves to the individual Western European countries instead of to NATO.

In the meantime, NATO had reacted with an expression of basic readiness for the proposed conference. In June 1970, the Warsaw Pact states took up the subject once again and accepted the GDR and West Germany as participants in such a conference as well as the United States and Canada. The following subjects were chosen for discussion: European security, renunciation of force, and questions of trade, science, technology and culture. The Western nations had shown themselves to be interested in such a conference only if a final category of cultural questions were included as a major topic. The United States was the power in the Western camp that had the greatest reservations about the conference, because it recognized only too clearly the motives of Moscow. These were not necessarily in accord with the readiness of the United States to approach concrete questions of cooperation.

There have been various opinions among the countries of the West with regard to the arrangements to be made for the ESC. Only at the NATO session in December 1971, was agreement on the basic policy achieved. The Berlin Agreement had to be signed between the Four Powers before any preliminary negotiations for the ESC could begin. At this meeting the representatives of the United States, Secretary of State William Rogers and Secretary of Defense Melvin Laird, made a decisive turn in the direction of the ESC. At the same time, it became clear however, that the United States had established a set of priorities for its East-West undertakings. The SALT talks headed the list. The MBFR talks were second, and finally came the ESC.

These developments led to the "diplomatic salon" —the multilateral talks—that gathered in Helsinki, Finland, in November 1972, to prepare for the Conference. What will become of this European Security Conference? Will it be another Congress of Vienna dictating a new international system in Europe, establish a kind of European United Nations, or be a peace conference à la Versailles?

The subjects for discussion suggested by the NATO countries show that they do not think the conference will turn out to be a peace conference à la Versailles. Security questions will be taken up as well as basic guidelines for relations between states and specific military questions. Freedom of movement for people and freedom of information and ideas as well as international cultural relations will be an important element of real détente. Among the problems that interest the European states as industrial nations, questions of trade, applied science and technology and research as well as the new concern for protection of the environment will provide material for negotiations at the ESC. The ESC must not be allowed to develop into a replay of the Versailles peace conference of 1919. In a similar sense, it would not be in the interests of the nations of Western Europe for the ESC to be institutionalized through long-term existence into a kind of European United Nations. The attraction of the concept of the United Nations has paled considerably in recent years anyway. To create such a regional system for Europe would only mean falling into the hands of the Soviet Union and its policy for Western Europe. Through such an organization, the Russians would gain an opportunity to involve themselves in all European affairs.

If the ESC is to bring détente, it must first of all be able to yield results through intensive negotiations as a conference of limited duration. The NATO communiqué from Lisbon spoke of *a* conference. But the efforts involved in such a conference cannot be justified by such vague proposals. Therefore, since it will clearly be impossible to resolve all important issues at one conference, it would seem practical to end the conference with the intention of calling it back into session at a later date after the necessary preparations.

A lasting European order, as was more or less achieved by the Congress of Vienna for the hundred years that followed, should not be expected as a result of the ESC. At the Congress of Vienna, delegations who thought the same way socially and ideologically were able to establish order over the heads of the peoples of Europe. In modern times—at least in the West—this has become impossible. On the basis of the contemporary political make-up as well, there are no architects of the same stuff as Metternich, who was responsible for the creation of that system. Neither Nixon nor Brezhnev nor even Pompidou or Brandt could achieve such a system today. The ambitions of the ESC must remain politically more modest if it wants to stimulate détente in Europe in practical terms.

A primary concern at the conference will be to guarantee some freedom of action to the states of Eastern Europe in spite of the strict controls implied in the Brezhnev Doctrine. Only if this status quo is replaced by freer movement can such a conference make sense. This increase in movement must take effect in terms of greater freedom for people, ideas, and information.

It is in the interest of the West that both the Western European states and the United States appear as partners at the MBFR and the ESC talks. All participants on the Western side must by now have realized that without a unified policy in the MBFR and ESC talks, Western objectives will not be reached. In the military dimension, they are NATO partners; on economic questions, most are Common Market members. In the basic confrontation between East and West, they are partners in the Atlantic Alliance. On the basis of these ties, they must continually maintain close consultation in order to counter any Soviet hopes of forcing loose the Western alliance. Under such conditions, it will be very clear to what extent the Soviet Union has looked at these negotiating sessions simply as propaganda instruments.

The West has a chance at the MBFR talks and the ESC to blunt the aggressive aspects of Soviet diplomacy. Through a unified position, it can demonstrate to the Soviet Union that détente politics in the seventies exists on the basis of a Western European unity and an Atlantic partnership with the United States. If the Soviet Union were to face up to this reality, surely record-breaking agreements could be made for the future of Europe.

Europe As a Nuclear Force

Not only the questions concerning American troop reductions, but also the Soviet-American SALT negotiations raise new issues concerning the "European nuclear force." SALT will remain a bipolar affair of the two nuclear giants. It is a sign of the decline of European influence that the allies of the United States must stand by to see what will come of it. As a result, rumors could arise that even the denuclearization of NATO might be a topic of the SALT negotiations and that the Europeans might, therefore, be stripped of all American nuclear protection. In this context, the "nuclear camaraderie" between the United States and the Soviet Union has once again been discussed. Since then the warnings of the Americans against bilateral negotiations between the European states and the Soviet Union have carried less weight. But as the first results have shown, the SALT talks are important for world peace and they should not be a source of such alarm in Europe.

Yet, SALT has had consequences for European security interests. On the one hand, in the wake of successful agreements at the level of the two giants, something could also be achieved for Europe in the conventional realm. On the other hand, at the nuclear level, concern for survival must lead to reflection on the potential for European initiatives of its own.

On the whole, the Soviet Union has achieved parity with the United States in strategic nuclear potential. Yet, it is still trying with resolute energy to go beyond this point and to surpass the United States.

Under these circumstances, the credibility of the American nuclear guarantee for Europe continues to decline. In fact, in view of America's current reflection on its role as the world's policeman, perhaps maintenance of a credible guarantee is too much to expect from the United States. It will, therefore, become more difficult for America to fulfill a basic condition of the strategy which Nixon described in his report to Congress in 1970: "The nuclear potential of our strategic as well as regional nuclear armed forces serves as a deterrent against an all-out Soviet attack on our European NATO allies or a Chinese attack on our Asian allies."

Therefore, in case of either success or failure, SALT can bring new tasks and problems for Western European cooperation in security politics. Despite efforts for collective action, security among the Western European allies retains a heavy national accent. This derives first of all from the fact that England and France are nuclear powers, and second from the unfavorable geographic position of West Germany. West Germany must therefore stimulate the thinking of its European allies along lines which will help to increase the collective nuclear protection.

Not distrust of America but a willingness for effective cooperation must provide the basis for an attempt to help to overcome the contradiction between America's policy towards Europe and its nuclear policy. It is realistic to comply with the American wish for a distribution of the burdens of conventional defense only if this process includes a sharing of the tasks in nuclear defense as well. It is meaningless that countries should prepare a currency union which is practically a common basis for their whole societal development but not attempt to do the same for the equally fundamental problem of security.

At the present, the question of nuclear protection for Western Germany seems to be anathema not only on the European scene but also for public opinion within West Germany itself. This is closely connected to a parallelled playing-down of conventional weapons protection as well. In the perception of Western Europeans, conventional war is frequently differentiated from nuclear war more strongly than is justifiable. In a conventional war today, the metropolitan areas of Western European industrial nations would suffer destruction in a way not essentially different from that which would result from a nuclear war. But to prevent war in any form in Europe and to find the most effective method of doing this is precisely the goal of all security politics. The proposition that conventional destruction can only be prevented by nuclear deterrence is still valid for Europe. Therefore, the extension of the nuclear strike potential of Britain and France as a second European deterrent in close cooperation with the United States would be in the good interests of Europe.

We are not talking about German nuclear weapons. All deliberations concerning a second nuclear pillar for Europe must be prefaced by the following understanding on the part of the Germans: West Germany is a middle-sized power; it should be neither too strong nor too weak. It has already become evident with respect to conventional weapons that the Western allies were not interested in a dominant Germany. German renunciation of nuclear weapons was one of the conditions for Germany's entry into the Western alliance. As is well known, as early as 1954, Adenauer was prepared to renounce the production of ABC (atomic, biological and chemical) weapons on the territory of West Germany. It was the policy of West Germany not to gain access to nuclear weapons in any way. Even today, when we see West Germany as a state with its own identity, we should not forget that it carries the burden of the German past into the present and the future. Nuclear weapons in Europe must be free of all claims from West Germany. Besides the declaration of 1954, it has proven its good will on the nuclear question by signing the Test Ban Treaty in 1963 and the Nuclear Non-Proliferation Treaty in 1968.

In signing the Nuclear Non-Proliferation Treaty, West Germany clarified its interpretation of the agreement in a nineteen-point supplementary note. It expressed its desire as an industrial nation not to be excluded from possible sources of atomic energy needed for modern industries. Yet, in this context it is more important to note that the German interpretation of the Nuclear Non-Proliferation Treaty left room for all kinds of European approaches to the relevant problems and that NATO was stressed as the basis of German security. At the same time, the Non-Proliferation Treaty does not stand in the way of solutions which might result from European-American cooperation.

A European nuclear defense could be achieved in two ways: first, through the development of a European nuclear armed force, and second, through Franco-British cooperation. In view of the trend towards the political unification of Europe, the prospect of an independent European nuclear protection force would, without doubt, be the more attractive one. It would be its task to prevent a siauation in which the Soviet Union could exert military pressure on Europe on the basis of Russian nuclear predominance. This would require the development of a European second-strike capacity powerful enough to respond to a Soviet first strike and, therefore, is with all probability impossible to rule out.

The second approach would involve the transformation of the existing nuclear potentials of France and Great Britain into second-strike capabilities. Such a solution might well be of particular interest to both England and France, since both are running the danger that their current nuclear potential will lose or not even achieve effective strength as a deterrent.

At the moment, however, neither country has the technological nor financial resources to make the changes necessary for an independent second-strike capability. Technological assistance from the United States and financial assistance from West Germany would have to be provided to such a project. They would also have to guarantee that this newly emerging nuclear defense potential would be geared into the political thinking of the West. British Prime Minister Edward Heath has already stated that such an enterprise "in trust for Europe" would promise success because the exchange of technological knowledge between France and England would enhance the overall potential. France's experiences and advantages in the construction of missiles would be meaningfully supplemented by British knowledge of nuclear warheads and especially by British achievements in the construction of Polaris submarines.

Thus, the Americans should not make any agreements during the continuing SALT negotiations which would rule out a proliferation of knowledge and experience to the French and British that could support the further development of their nuclear capabilities.

Political alarm stimulated by such a project for an independent European nuclear force could be mitigated by a statement on the part of West Germany clearly renouncing control over nuclear weapons. Such a statement could also have a beneficial effect on European détente politics.

In this context, the West Germany would have to insist on two conditions:

1] West Germany could support the development of a joint Franco-British nuclear force only if the United States were a participant in the project. An exclusively European project as a one-to-one substitute for the American guarantee would in no way represent the security interests of Germany. The function of such a European nuclear force would consist solely in backing up the credibility of the American deterrent, because a nuclear war in Europe in which the Americans remain neutral is a politically unthinkable prospect.

2] West Germany would have to insist that the establishment of all-European nuclear force not be tied in any way to: *a)* a German withdrawal from NATO, or *b)* the withdrawal of all tactical nuclear weapons from the territory of West Germany. Neither of these prospects would be compatible with the goal of a stable European defense since in both cases the security of West Germany would be severely compromised.

For all parties involved, the decisive factor in the establishment of a new European nuclear force, if one were to be established, would have to be a recognition of the fact that war in Europe has become impossible and détente politics are the only alternative left to the Continent. Peace in Europe has not been preserved through the harmony of peaceful intentions in East and West, but by the balance of the military powers. This will continue to be the case in the future as long as détente in Europe has not yet become a reality.

13

The Monetary Crisis in International Affairs

The development of Western democracies in the future will be determined by their political and military security as well as by the growth of their economies. For every liberal order, the framework of its development is provided by its military and political security; the means of its development, by its economy. America has been the leading power of the Western world both by guaranteeing security with its nuclear capabilities and by assuring the stability and growth of the Western economies with the dollar as the leading currency.

In both domestic and international politics, consideration of economic issues has moved to a priority position. The capability of the traditional state to develop its economy with its own means has become increasingly limited. Economic and social development require comprehensive multilateral cooperation and an exchange of ideas as well as goods with other countries. Therefore, economic issues have become an essential element of alliance relationships. Economic relations cannot be separated from political relations, and just as war cannot be left to the generals alone, neither can economic questions be left to the economists alone.

Henry Kissinger made this point emphatically when he pointed out that America could not pursue a confrontation with Europe on trade and monetary issues for very long without at the same time initiating a beginning of the disintegration of the Atlantic Alliance. Steps towards such a disintegration of the Alliance could arise as a result of a deterioration in the economic relations among the partners. Such a move, he said, would play into the hands of the Soviets and their particular plan for détente.

What we call the "world economic system" today is, from a political point of view, basically the cooperative effort in international economics and trade between and among the non-Communist states. This effort is primarily regulated by the Group of Ten made up of the major Western financial powers (the United States, Britain, Canada, Sweden, Japan, France, Germany, Italy, Belgium and The Netherlands) that are involved in most of the international borrowing and lending arrangements. (Switzerland participates as an observer.) Thus, any crisis in the world economic system is essentially a crisis of the Western world.

Even during the first years of the seventies, monetary crises have been so frequent that the need for a new currency agreement has constantly increased. All Western industrial societies have become worried not only about the foreign exchange value of their currencies and inflation in their domestic economies, but also about the effects on their own economies of the international economic policies of other countries. Even in West Germany, renowned as an economically and politically stable country, the mark has lost 40 per cent of its value within the last two decades. The crisis of the world monetary system and worldwide inflation could very easily destroy the intricate network of international trade which originated in the postwar period and has grown by billions of dollars. As our experience during the thirties taught us, drastic protectionist measures of economic nationalism very soon have unfavorable effects on the economic, social and also the political sectors of not only the country that initiates such measures but on all of its trading partners as well. Finally, if we consider the renaissance of Marxism which rejects the free market economy anyway, we quickly recognize that contemporary problems of transatlantic trade and monetary flows might eventually put the stability of the Western democracies themselves to the test.

For a long time, the stability of transatlantic economic relations was considered a secure underpinning of the Western Alliance. America provided the Europeans not only with security through its military power but also with affluence through its economic power. As the developments of the last years have shown, an economic boom in the Western European countries has developed parallel to the Continent's continued need for military support from the United States. But at the same time, the economic success of the European economies is also raising a number of questions about trade and monetary policy within the Alliance, and these questions, in fact, have led to problems that have become the center of attention in Atlantic relations today. With the dollar as the leading currency, the Americans influenced the economic development of the Western world decisively. John Connally, former United States Secretary of the Treasury, described the situation in the following way: "For many years the United States stood like Atlas, firmly supporting the stability of the world monetary system."

For a long period after the end of World War II, this dominating role of the dollar was the most typical instance of American hegemony in international economic relations. America also carried the major part of the responsibility for a stable world economy. In the pursuit of its dominating monetary and economic functions, America energetically supported the establishment of the World Bank (International Bank for Reconstruction and Development) and the International Monetary Fund, the Marshall Plan, several international foreign aid programs and the creation of GATT (General Agreement on Tariffs and Trade) and the OECD (Organization for Economic Cooperation and Development) as well as the establishment of economic and monetary assistance for the Third World. Yet in recent years, the leading position of the dollar has been shaken by the growing deficit in the American balance of payments. This crisis has developed as the economic and social problems of the United States have grown and as the Europeans have come to consider America's negative balance of payments as an important factor contributing to the growing inflation in their own countries.

The Monetary Crisis Is an Alliance Crisis

No language was spared in describing the monetary crisis of 1971. At first, there was talk about a trade and currency war between the Common Market and the United States. In Europe, some critics declared the Common Market was dead. Worried prophets who predicted the rise of a world economic crisis echoed their fear. When President Nixon announced the American measures of August 1971, an advisor to the American

President said: "This will be the most important weekend in economic history since March 4, 1933." He was comparing Nixon's speech to President Roosevelt's inaugural announcement of the New Deal. When the Group of Ten reached agreement at its Washington conference at the end of 1971—the so-called Smithsonian Agreement—President Nixon called this consensus "the most important agreement on currency in the history of the world." The importance of the crisis and of the attempts at its solution were thus emphasized once again. But then in 1972 and 1973, other monetary crises occurred.

Since imperial times and before 1914, strict adherence to the gold standard necessitated little international political concern about world monetary matters. The international politics of monetary policy are, therefore, a relatively recent development in relations among the nations of the world. In the post-World War II period, international monetary policy was derived from the system established under the leadership of the United States at Bretton Woods.

The heart of this monetary system was the dollar and the confidence of the Western world in the economic power of the United States. The currencies of the participating countries were based on gold and on foreign currencies, particularly the dollar, which made up foreign exchange reserves for the participating countries. The dollar had this leading function because it was the only currency that was convertible into gold. The exchange rate was 35 dollars per ounce of gold, a price that had been pegged in 1934. The Bretton Woods agreement established fixed exchange rates and the extensive convertibility of the most important currencies. To keep the system functioning and to be able to give credits to the participating countries, coordination of international monetary and credit policy was established by the setting up of the World Bank and the World Monetary Fund. International monetary policy was the responsibility of the Fund. The Bank was responsible for elaborating and administering international credit policy.

This system was highly successful in reconstructing national economies and world trade after World War II. In the early years, the dollar was much in demand. The participating trading nations were never able to satisfy their demand for this currency. They all needed it to pay for American goods, since at this time the United States was the most sought-after supplier in the world. Then with the recovery of their economies, the European countries themselves became attractive trade partners for America. The dollar flowed into Europe through a variety of channels, including American investments, expenditures for American troops in Europe, and via those countries of the Third World which received American foreign aid for military and developmental purposes and which were paying for their European imports with dollars. We should also not forget the steadily increasing expenditures of American tourists in Europe.

By the beginning of the sixties, the American balance of payment had reversed itself; it showed a deficit. European central banks began to hoard the dollar and the gold. United States gold reserves in Fort Knox dropped from $22.8 billion in 1950 to $10 billion at the beginning of the seventies. The central banks of the European Community countries had accumulated reserves in gold and dollars that amounted to $31.2 billion, whereas in 1950 they had held only $3.1 billion. The situation might be compared to that of the casino bank which provides a group of losing bettors with chips to gamble with. Soon, because the group of individuals is winning, the stakes have grown beyond all expectations, and suddenly the bank has to declare itself broke. Most of the chips are in the hands of players who only recently were in the bank's debt.

As late as 1968, the former United States Secretary of the Treasury Henry Fowler described the value of the American dollar in the following terms: "Gold is the sun and the dollar is the moon—the distance between them is unchangeable." But only a few years later, at the beginning of the seventies, the situation was judged in more sober terms by Paul A. Samuelson, the American winner of the first Nobel Prize awarded for economics: "For more than a decade, the dollar has been an overvalued currency." Slowly an economic and political problem has arisen over just how much the dollar could still decline in value without being rejected as the international means of payment. Already in 1968 only every fourth dollar was covered by gold. This means that the position of the dollar as a world monetary reserve was, in effect, sustained almost solely by the political prestige of the United States. Europeans became critical of the increasing inflationary influence of the dollar in Europe.

A result of the chronic deficit in the American balance of payments during the sixties was an enormous amount of dollars floating around in Europe at the beginning of the seventies. Amounting to almost $50 billion, these so-called Eurodollars were floating in the monetary markets. At any point in time, they could endanger any national currency by their fast inflow or outflow which was particularly facilitated by their unrestricted convertibility. At first, the emerging dangers were politically contained. The Americans were able to induce the European central banks not to exchange their dollars for gold by promising a reduction in the deficit in the balance of payments of the United States. Finally, in 1971, it became clear that the deficit was growing steadily worse instead of being reduced.

The economies of Western European countries which owed their original recovery primarily to the dollar were now running the risk of encountering substantial crises of their own as a result of the same dollar. A quotation attributed to Lenin was making the rounds: "To destroy bourgeois society, it is necessary to devastate its monetary system."

Finally, on August 15, 1971, Nixon announced the measures his administration would take to solve the monetary crisis. They had an explosive effect in America and around the world. The dollar convertibility into gold was ended, and a series of temporary protectionist measures were introduced to protect the American economy. Among these measures was a 10 per cent rebate from taxes paid on investment goods made in the U.S. and a 10 per cent surcharge on foreign imports. For the American economy proper, Nixon prescribed a ninety-day wage and price freeze as the first phase of a comprehensive new economic policy. The net effect of the Nixon move was to make the dollar a paper currency.

Public opinion in the United States and Europe regarding the Nixon announcement reflected a considerable poisoning of the psychological climate among the Western allies. These feelings were expressed by sentiments of anti-Americanism on one side and isolationism on the other. It was another example of just how easily misunderstandings arising in the economic sphere can have a disintegrating effect on the international political sphere. But at the end of the year, the Western governments got busy, and lively diplomatic activity to overcome the crisis began. Besides the conferences of the Group of Ten and the OECD sessions, summit meetings of heads of state were scheduled, aiming at a settlement of the crisis. Special note should be given to the talks between French Premier Pompidou and Chancellor Brandt and to the summit meeting between Nixon and Pompidou in the Azores. Both meetings signalized the emergence of solutions to the monetary crisis.

President Nixon reserved for himself the privilege of announcing the results of the Smithsonian agreement on money and trade of December 18, 1971. As he announced the devaluation of the dollar, and the revaluation of a number of Western currencies, including the German mark, he also pointed out that all countries had made concessions. The Canadians were to continue to float their dollar, and Britain and France were to retain the existing exchange rates of their currencies. Tied to these measures was an American promise to reduce import duties and eliminate the surcharge.

This agreement changed the international monetary system as laid down in Bretton Woods in three basic respects. The upper and lower limits of permitted exchange fluctuations were expanded considerably. Since basically the principle of fixed exchange rate continues to be valid, this means that the gain was more flexibility in decisions concerning revaluation and devaluation of currencies. The dollar lost some of its importance as a reserve currency because it was no longer to be exchanged for gold by the United States Treasury. Therefore, in the future, the so-called "special drawing rights" of the World Monetary Fund, which had been agreed upon by the Group of Ten in 1968, were to take over the role as a leading international reserve asset instead. Finally, the most startling measure was that, for the first time since 1934, the gold parity of the dollar was changed. What this meant for Americans can perhaps best be evaluated if we keep in mind the fact that the changes of 1971 came out of arrangements that had been based on the value of the dollar in 1934.

The London *Times* saw in the agreement resulting from the Washington meeting an important turning point in the political relations of the United States with the rest of the non-Communist world. It presumed that the United States would now act less as a leading power and more as a participant concerned with its specifically national interest in future monetary trade and political questions.

> In this way, the other members will rediscover that the United States still holds a powerful tactical position. During the first twenty-five years of the postwar era, this power was exercised with moderation and with a true feeling of international responsibility in the monetary as well as the military realm. From now on, there will be a much greater American preparedness to employ tactical strength to guarantee its short-range national interests.

The Western world will have to be prepared to consider this point about the national interests of the United States in looking at future economic relations. People knowledgeable about America have always been surprised how strongly the American business community is oriented towards its domestic market, in spite of America's extensive international commitments. But it is also to the advantage of the Western world that the United States no longer dominates the world economy to the degree that it has until recently. It used to be said that when America sneezes, Europe catches cold. But in 1970 it was evident that symptoms of a crisis in the American economy were not immediately transmitted throughout the Western world. The balance between the United States and Europe has shifted. As a result, the Western world is now involved in establishing its economy on two pillars.

This must be taken into account in looking at broader considerations relating to a reordering of the international economic system. Any discussion will have to cover the formation of a European currency union which, besides Europe, will also include the sterling countries and Africa, balanced by a dollar bloc formed by the United States, Canada and Latin America. The question of how or where to fit Japan into this arrangement would also have to be decided. The question is, however, would the formation of these two monetary blocs make good sense?

There is reason to doubt the general political expediency in constructing two such monetary blocs. There are particularly intra-European doubts concerning such a currency bloc. One point of view was articulated by Valéry Giscard d'Estaing, French Finance Minister, when he stated that France would not be prepared to exchange the hegemony of the dollar for the hegemony of the German mark. More promising for the future and also politically more satisfying would be the establishment of an Atlantic free-trade zone including Japan. This effort would involve the restructuring of the monetary system to contain fixed parties, increased flexibility, and above all independence from any single national economy. Special drawing rights are today generally recognized as capable of playing a major role in the new system. The eminent German banker, Hermann

Abs, characterized the importance of this innovation in monetary policy with the slogan: "Put the paper tiger into your bank."

Trade relations between the United States, Europe and Japan must be restructured. As a precondition for the Atlantic free-trade area, the establishment of a European currency and economic union would be an important step in achieving an equitable balance between the United States and Europe.

The Common Market and the United States: Partners or Rivals?

Americans are characteristically impatient people. They have expected far too much from the development of a united Europe. Former American Under Secretary of State George Ball's complaint that the political unification of Europe has remained bogged down in basic problems and that economic integration is not yet complete is an example of this mood. At the same time, there has been a certain change in the point of view of the United States. With regard to the Common Market, American negotiators are more likely to speak of competition than of cooperation. Servan-Schreiber has written, "Europe founded a common market, but no international power." The Americans wanted to help in the building of a "United States of Europe." But they see a merchant's society and club of protectionists in the works, interested in making money while enjoying the protection of the United States. The Americans have pointed out to the Western Europeans, as they have to the Japanese as well, that political responsibility must be tied to economic power. They feel that greater burdens of the Western Alliance should be carried by all.

In fact, the Common Market has been a considerable economic success, and there can be no doubt but that this economic success has political significance. But the Americans are right when they claim that hopes for speedy political unification have diminished rather than grown. One hoped at the founding of the Common Market that it would develop a dynamic character of its own by means of which the mechanism of economic integration would automatically pull political cooperation after it. But the economic success of what Chancellor Erhard once called "the most daring and resolute experiment" has become a subject of political controversy in Europe and even in international politics.

With the reduction of customs barriers and impediments to trade, the Western European states have been successful in achieving economic development leading to a higher standard of living for all of its members. From national economies with underemployment there have developed industrial states with full employment, foreign exchange surpluses, and ever-increasing foreign trade. By the end of the sixties, Common Market exports of industrial products were twice as high as those of the United States. Nevertheless, the Americans were still profiting from the growth of the Common Market. It was their fastest growing market. Since 1958, the volume of trade between the United States and the Common Market has tripled, and American exports to the Common Market have increased at an above average rate.

It is irrelevant to American aversions to the Common Market that the country's balance of trade with the Market remained positive during a time when American exports had already lost their competitive position in international markets. But then in 1971, for the first time since 1893, the United States had a deficit in its balance of trade. For a while, the Americans could still point to a positive balance of $1.3 billion in trade with the Common Market. But when the overall deficit in the American balance of trade went over $6 billion in 1972, the Americans suffered a deficit in the balance of trade with the Common Market for the first time. It is not fair to equate Japanese-American trade with European-American trade, as Americans often do, for the reason that there has been a continuing high deficit in the balance of trade with Japan for some time, while the trade balance with the Common Market has been mostly positive except for 1972.

The list of complaints and the threats the United States has made against the Common Market is quite striking. But in Brussels, American demands for an improvement of American trade with Europe have been reacted to with bitter criticism. In a comment on the scope of the American demands, a highly placed official said: "The only other thing the Americans could ask us to do is to give up any further expansion of the Market." The European Community was particularly hard-hit by the American demands for liberalizing the Common Market agricultural policies. It has been in this area that the Common Market has been able to achieve agreement within the Community only with the greatest difficulty, difficulty that has included at times even the possible collapse of the organization. For this reason, a sudden change in the Market's agricultural policy is hardly feasible. It would only be possible in the course of several years. American demands in the realm of Common Market preferential policy with regard to other states would also only be realizable with great difficulty. This refers to the preferential trade treaties which the Common Market has concluded with the neutral members of EFTA (European Free Trade Association), the former French and English colonies in Africa, and states bordering on the Mediterranean. The Americans have demanded a return to the principle of the most favored nation as negotiated in the Kennedy Round of GATT trade negotiations between 1962 and 1967.

Just how closely politics and trade are tied together is shown fully in the problem of the states bordering on the Mediterranean. The Common Market states concluded a series of special agreements with the countries of the Mediterranean to provide political support for these states by economic preferences. Look, for example, at the North African states like Morocco and Algeria that arose from the French colonial empire or at the NATO members in the eastern Mediterranean region (Greece and Turkey). What the Europeans see as economic and political support for these countries, the United States sees as discrimination. This American reaction is largely motivated by the substantial security commitment the United States has made to these countries in the Mediterranean area.

No observer of the United States has any doubts any more that protectionist tendencies have been on the increase in America. Recently, the protectionist campaigns of the unions have become particularly explicit, and can be seen in their solid support for the Foreign Trade and Investment Act (the so-called Burke-Hartke legislation), which one American newspaper characterized as "the most restrictive piece of protectionist legislation to reach the Congress since 1930."

Congressional sentiment for protectionism has also been growing, particularly in light of the U.S. balance of trade deficits in 1971 and 1972. It also seems as if the White House has been reacting favorably to this trend. When, for example, the President of the United States demands "fair conditions" for American exports, it sounds like a threat to use the country's "big stick": the setting up of American trade barriers against imports from Europe unless. . . .

Immediately after the devaluation of the dollar in 1973, Representative Wilbur Mills, Chairman of the House Ways and Means Committee, where trade legislation originates, called for a surcharge of 15 per cent on all imports as an additional step to be taken by the United States. These demands are still ringing in the ears of Europeans. Naturally, demands such as these have not been the determining factor in the American government's diplomacy in Europe. But they have given rise to a concern that the United States might resort to a negotiating tactic that would tie the demand for a liberalization of world trade with a threat of protectionism.

The Common Market is very susceptible. The demand for a reduction of tariffs poses a difficult problem for the Common Market. The question before it is maintenance of the joint tariffs on products from outside the Market since such joint tariffs play such an important role in holding the member nations together. The Europeans are convinced that the Americans are not really so disadvantaged in the agricultural sector with regard to the balance of trade, or even in the area of tariffs. What is noteworthy with regard to customs, one frequently hears, is that in the Common Market the average tariff runs at about 6 per cent, whereas it is 7.1

per cent in the United States and 9.7 per cent in Japan. Europeans also point out that with regard to quantitative limits, about 20 per cent of the American customs categories but only 4.3 per cent of the European ones are still subject to such restrictions. The next round of GATT negotiations will be particularly concerned with achieving a further reduction of such trade barriers.

Yet there is no gainsaying the fact that there has been a decline in American exports to the Common Market countries. It is generally pointed out in European business circles that the decline in imports from America during 1971 and 1972 was due largely to the instability of the international monetary system. Furthermore, it has also been suggested that this decline has been the result of a reaction on the part of the Europeans to the restrictive customs tactics employed by the Americans. But it is important to note that, as in the past, the Common Market remains the most important market for American agricultural products. Even in 1972, agricultural exports from the United States to Europe increased by 10 per cent.

When Henry Kissinger announced the interest of the Nixon administration in the development of a new Atlantic Charter in a speech in New York in the spring of 1973, it was appropriate for him to say: "We have profited from the economic integration of Europe as have the countries of that continent. Increased trade within Europe has fostered the growth of the economies of all the European states as well as the expansion of trade in both directions across the Atlantic."

Another important argument for the Europeans results from a special phenomenon of modern economics. American business has developed a new strategy of international production, and in many cases this new element in the world economy has had a considerable impact on traditional American exports to Europe. For a variety of reasons beginning in the 1950s, American firms have gone abroad to manufacture the same products they make at home. For Servan-Schreiber, these American firms—the so-called multinational corporations—with their vast financial and other resources in Europe have become the "American challenge" to the native companies of the European countries.

Of course, these foreign investments made by American companies have their effect on the balance of payments situation of the United States. Not only do the military and development aid given by the United States contribute to its balance of payments deficit but also these foreign investments made by American firms. Naturally, if Europeans can buy computers, electronic and electrical equipment, tractors and other products from American affiliates on the Continent itself, they will no longer import from the United States. Therefore, American companies in Europe have also contributed to the decline in exports from the United States. In 1970, one billion dollars were transferred from American affiliates in Common Market states to their headquarters offices in the United States. But in the same year, for the first time, IBM made a larger profit through its foreign sales than it did in the United States itself.

Henry Ford has suggested a new vision for the United States along this perspective. "Let us leave industrial undertakings to the others," he recommended, "and we shall become a service nation." He has already started along this path with his compact car, the "Pinto." This car has a German motor, British gear mechanism, and a Mexican electronic system. The end product is put together in Canada. These strengths of

American know-how and management appear to ensure for the present and the future not only the overcoming of the current difficulties but also the consolidation of America's leading role in an expanding world economy.

The problems just delineated have mainly concerned relations between the United States and the Common Market states. But just as was the case with regard to politics and security, the special nature of German-American relations is also apparent in this area. Look at the three goals of the United States in connection with international financial questions: a readjustment of international currency exchange rates, improved conditions for American trade with the Common Market countries, and a new division of the burdens of Western defense. It is clear that these demands are directed towards West Germany in particular. Every two years, West Germany concludes a foreign exchange agreement with the United States that provides a balance payment of marks for American military expenditures in Germany. The last agreement was concluded in 1971 and involved a balance payment of 6.65 billion marks.

Another example of the importance of the German role in the international monetary system and its support of the American dollar is the succession of revaluations the mark has gone through in recent months. As an export nation par excellence—exporting more than one-third of the production of its key industries—West Germany is heavily dependent on the openness of the American market. A member of the board of the Volkswagen company commented: "VW exports without the American market are just as unimaginable as an American automobile market without the VW." But precision mechanical tools, optical products, office machines, computers, as well as heavy machinery and chemicals also figure heavily in German exports to the United States. Any increase in the cost of, or cut in, the quantity of German exports to America would very quickly have a substantial impact on the German economy. If one acknowledges the fact of these German trade interests, the burdens carried by West Germany in defense and international monetary affairs, and the balance of trade between Germany and America which remains tilted in favor of the Germans, then it is clear that the German–American relationship plays an important role in transatlantic economic relations.

In this connection, any conflicts between the Common Market and the United States have a particular bearing on West Germany. It is clear in Europe and in America that all-embracing and continuous consultations and negotiations are necessary to solve these problems. The results of these negotiations will contribute to developments in Europe during the coming years. Both big powers, the United States and the Soviet Union, are alert observers of the Common Market developments. The Americans are concerned about their trade situation; the Russians fear that the success of the Common Market will lead to political unification. The Americans were ready to take the economic disadvantages of these political developments in stride because they could then hope for a resulting, much-needed sharing of burdens. The Russians, on the other hand, could be satisfied with the current situation if they had to, since it contains little momentum in the direction of political unification, but allows for widened trade with the Soviet Union.

It will be interesting to see which of the two world powers has its expectations confirmed. The new pickup in trade with the East could be of considerable political importance. It will also be interesting to see, in light of the talks by officials of the United States Commerce Department in Moscow, just how ready the United States is to participate in the economic development of the Soviet Union with its own investment capital. Were one to combine all of the projects in the Soviet Union which Japan, the United States, and Europe are considering financing, one could easily visualize an aid program just as extensive as the historic Marshall Plan. The German journalist Thomas Wybraniec pointed out in the *Frankfurter Allgemeine Zeitung* that long-term credits that have already been granted or promised to the Soviet Union by West Germany, France, Great Britain, and Italy amount to some nine billion marks. A much-discussed question in the future will be whether such credits can be given without political overtones. Western businessmen in Europe and America are burning to get at the Eastern market. Their readiness to support a conciliatory *Ostpolitik* on the part of their governments has grown. Nevertheless, they want more security for their economic involvement.

The convergence of international economics and international politics is not a particularly comfortable development from the Western point of view. In the future, however, politicians must pursue both increasingly in East–West relations. It will be a question of producing economic ties under conditions that actually encourage a peaceful balancing process between states with differing political, social, and economic systems. Within the Western Alliance, efforts must be made to avoid endangering past close relations through economic competition.

From its inception, the German-American relationship has not been based only on political and security issues. Even if somewhat one-sided at that time, it has always been an economic alliance. This economic aspect will continue to play a major role in the future as well. It will be a major task of politics within the Western Alliance to prevent economic crises in the member countries that produce the larger part of the total gross national product of the Western world. But economic crises are not only Alliance crises. Seen from the inside of the states concerned, they are also crises of democracy. For this reason, in the last analysis, economic cooperation in the Western Alliance contributes to the stability of all the democratic systems of the world.

14

From the Industrial
to the Post-Industrial Society

"An industrial society devotes itself to the production of goods, and in this sense capitalism and socialism are two varieties of industrial society that are only different with regard to private property relations and the centers that make decisions on the allocation of investment funds. The post-industrial society, on the other hand, is organized around knowledge and skills. This fact leads to new societal relations and to new structures that must be organized politically." These definitions are offered to us by sociologist Daniel Bell.

Gradually, societies will move from the production of goods to the provision of services. But today the only country in the world in which the service sector of the economy already contains more than half of all persons employed and produces more than half of the gross national product is the United States. The countries of Western Europe are also coming closer to this economic threshold. About 40 per cent of all those employed in Western Europe are already working in the service sector.

What is a "service economy"? In 1956 the number of white-collar workers in the United States for the first time became larger than that of blue-collar workers. As a result of the changes in the class structure of America today, for every four blue-collar workers there are five white-collar workers. Thus, with the machines of the technological age, a new society is emerging whose technical organization will be characterized by the capacity of its members for management and whose communities will be guided by novel social concepts. Of course, the conditions of industrial society must first be realized before this new development becomes a possibility.

It is apparent that a country can become an atomic power more easily than an industrial power. Even the so-called "threshold powers" such as Brazil and India come closer to the former status than the latter. But in these cases there are just as few real impulses for post-industrial development as in the Communist-ruled nations of Eastern Europe. Those countries are industrial nations, but they fall short of the necessary level for the next step in their production and management experience.

When Western Europe looks at other societies to find standards for its own development, it always returns to the model provided by the United States. But it cannot allow itself to be troubled by the current problems in America. In all of those aspects of their existence, the Europeans are well aware of their close ties to the Americans. The successes that the United States achieves in its post-industrial development will also influence Europe. "The revolution is coming from the United States. It is a revolution that is based on neither Marx nor Jesus, and one that will bring new patterns of behavior to the world." This is the prophecy of the French political commentator Jean-Francois Revel, who has received considerable attention in the United States.

"The revolution of the twentieth century will emanate from the United States. It can only happen there and it has already begun. It will only spread across the rest of the world once it has been successful in the United States."

Revel has his own idea of just what such a revolution involves, but he has seen elements throughout American society that are pressing out and beyond national borders and that make up a tendency towards a trans-national society. This tendency is growing regardless of state borders or geographical location. Servan-Schreiber saw a danger to Europe in the worldwide expansion of American technology and methods of economic management. At the same time, however, he realized that national borders have become an obstacle to the progress of the technological revolution when he wrote: "Areas such as scientific research, airplane construction, space research, and the computer industry require a level of economic development that is beyond the grasp of the domestic situations of the medium powers."

But Servan-Schreiber's thinking remains too strongly focused on the areas of technology and management and also is too strictly limited to the European context which he wants to see sharply delimited from the United States. His concern that Europe could become an American dependency is less relevant today than the European concern that the United States might isolate itself too much from its allies on the Continent. Europe's relationship with America will not be determined by its fear of the superiority of American technology or its competition with American trade, but only by the common concern over the future of Western industrial society and its democratic development.

There is a gap between Europe and the United States in the provision of public services and the principle of the socially enlightened state. Here we can point to a kind of "attitude gap" on the basis of which the Europeans are further advanced than the Americans.

Thus, there is a certain juxtaposition of the technological lead of the United States supported above all by well-financed research efforts and the institutions and patterns of behavior of the Europeans that have developed through strong public involvement in socially enlightened societies. Post-industrial society must provide both elements to its members.

Surely the synthesis that is suggested here is a good basis for further cooperation. Even today, it has become clear that our preparations for the future go far beyond the organizational problems of public services and production. Not only have the living conditions of people in industrial society changed rapidly, the industrial society itself has also provoked conditions that threaten the existence of man. Our scientific and technological civilization has resulted in an industrial society in which the balance between technological progress and the fulfillment of basic human needs is not always maintained. In fact, the general tendency seems to be that technological progress develops a dynamic tempo of its own that has all too little relation to the needs of human existence. It has already become a question of whether what is called "progress" is in the true service of man.

Disenchantment with industrial society has become a mood that is characteristic of our time. In Europe we see increasingly how progress towards the full condition of industrial society seems to be synonymous with a kind of "Americanization." In many instances, expression of anti-Americanism is merely an expression of disenchantment with the conditions of industrial society, a sign of the urgent wish to escape from what the German political scientist Richard Löwenthal has referred to as "intellectual Ludditism." (The Luddites were groups of workmen in early nineteenth century England who organized to destroy manufacturing machinery in the belief that its use diminished employment.) But simply to say, "the whole business just doesn't please me at all" is hardly an appropriate answer to the problems of industrial society. One can hardly conceive of any other way of living in the highly developed states of today.

The basic subject for all who are politically concerned today is the quality of life in industrial society and the way in which this lifestyle should be developed in the future. As he proceeds into post-industrial society, man must rearrange his life in such a way so as not to destroy but constantly improve the progress he makes both in his methods of production and his techniques of approaching the problems of society.

Unemployment, caused by a combination of decreased need for manpower and overeducation of segments of the population, and environmental pollution caused by advanced technology are problems which call for immediate attention. In addition, sophisticated medical advances have increased man's life expectancy, and modern society must find a useful place for its older citizens. The most difficult question of all is why an advanced technological society cannot provide an equal standard of living for all its people. Underprivileged minorities must be brought up to the level of the majority who have attained a comfortable standard of living.

These problems of an industrial society all come

together as components in the search for the better living conditions which are increasingly becoming the main concern of all politics. In this context, free and democratic political methods stand before new challenges. To the extent that politics remain important to the life of the individual, liberal processes of agreement in a democracy become more necessary than ever before. Only if the methods of the government remain dependent on the support of those affected and all of the groups of society take part in the decisions will assurances be possible that technological progress will lead to new possibilities and freedom for all segments of the society. Only a political system that allows all of the people affected to determine the extent, the tempo, and the goals of modern development can offer such a guarantee.

More participation by the people in the government is, therefore, necessary for political life in Western democracies. He who wishes further developments along liberal lines can only work within the system, for only it allows for both criticism and change at the same time. Democratic institutions such as a Parliament or a Presidential office are not ends in themselves. They are open to criticism on the basis of their achievements or lack of achievements or even on the basis of their composition. They should be judged on the basis of their effectiveness.

Without doubt, life in the Western democracies offers the most attractive political and social circumstances available in our time for the people of our time. Its great powers of attraction, above all to peoples of the Communist countries of Europe, cannot be questioned. A basic reason for all of this is that the people of a Western democracy expect the system to deliver. It is judged on the achievements of today and not on its promises for the future time. Here and now is what matters. Of course, this can lead to excesses, to efforts to deal with everything at once without really solving any one thing, and to impatience. It can also lead to a neglect of the future.

Today, the societies most plagued with self-doubt are to be found in the West. At the threshold of a new post-industrial status, many must constantly postpone the ultimate successful transition because of constantly arising difficulties. At the same time, however, communism and socialism continue to be extolled with messianic conviction and with hymns singing of an idyllic future. Will the self-doubting West succumb to these melodious tunes as time goes by? Or will we be able to stick resolutely to the tasks demanded of us by our future? Philosopher Karl Popper sees the main conflict of our time as one between rationalism and irrationalism. In fact, for him, this is the basic moral question man faces.

It is unimaginable that the answers to the challenges of the future will be different in each Western country or that any of the answers can be implemented in one state independently of the others.

The Agenda for Western Policy

The financial, political, and military efforts undertaken by West Germany in the context of the Western Alliance will only be worthwhile if the effects of the Alliance on military security also have a broader impact on the social stability and further development of the Western democracies. Nor should the efforts made in pursuit of détente be allowed to pose any obstacle to this process. Great Britain's entry into the Common Market and the negotiations between the United States and the European Community over trade relations will coincide with the conferences on arms limitation and European security in Vienna and Helsinki. These conferences could easily stretch on through the seventies. There is, of course, a chance they might even have an increasingly strong effect on European politics, while the concepts of European unity and the Atlantic partnership gradually lose their priority in the political thinking of the countries of the Western Alliance. The Alliance runs the risk of becoming an armored consumer club without any standard of set political goals. One possible scenario for the coming years of the seventies might well be a community of Western European states, each ruled by socialists including François Mitterand, Pietro Nenni, Erhard Eppler, and Harold Wilson. Such a Europe could be expected to show a greater readiness to give up the European-Atlantic concept in favor of an all-Europe-Soviet approach.

The stability of the Western democracies and their Alliance is the basis for the politics of peace in the seventies. It will be necessary for the survival of the Alliance through this decade, however, to once again explicitly articulate the set of commonly held Western foreign policy goals that threatened to come apart during the sixties. These goals should be based on a recognition of three factors which should provide the underpinnings for relations between states in the 1970s: a concern for human life in industrial society, technological development on the way to the post-industrial society, and efforts for the maintenance of peace. All are tied together in this complex world. It is impossible to have one without the other.

A pooling of Western technical know-how and

scientific knowledge would help to strengthen the potential of the social policies of the Western democracies. A precondition to the achievement of this not undramatic prospect quite clearly is the maintenance of peace. Joint efforts for the achievement of détente as well as shared preparations for defense form a part of this task. American and Western European efforts on a worldwide scale to help the developing countries are also vital to maintenance of peace. Naturally, there is hope that Eastern Europe will also join in this project as in the politics of détente and, finally, in the common experience of the development of industrial society.

But the West cannot wait for this to happen. In fact, with its own resources, the West must undertake societal developments in the Third World which would insure conditions of freedom in the countries of the Third World. Preservation of this freedom must continue to remain a central theme of Western policy. Such a theme will provide a broad basis for future cooperative efforts that must take place in joint undertakings in the politics of détente, in models and programs for post-industrial society, in aid to developing countries and adequate defense arrangements as well as in the creation of institutions and the development of methods for further cooperation and consultation.

The Western world must set up its own agenda for its joint efforts. Henry Kissinger was right when he urged in his New York speech that the Atlantic problems be handled in an all-embracing context. We must get away from the habit of thinking in terms of separate boxes through which defense problems, trade problems, monetary problems, and questions related to the political development of a society can only be dealt with separately.

Already in 1969, cooperation was begun in addressing the tasks facing modern societies. Related projects were initiated within the framework of NATO on such subjects as transportation safety, the prevention of sea pollution, relief in case of natural catastrophe, and urban problems. All Western industrial societies have very similar problems in different degrees, but a single state can hardly deal with the ones it is facing alone. And, of course, some of these problems such as sea pollution are not just intrastate problems but are interstate and international problems. This realization must lead to an organization for the solution of these problems based on a division of the problems and a division of labor. Another important problem area for a cooperative solution is the question of providing energy to the Western industrial states. Technological cooperation must become the object of far-reaching diplomatic efforts. In this case, once again, it would not be right to leave the efforts to the specialists alone. The subject of technological cooperation should be taken up in future top-level consultations as well.

Joint projects in such social policy areas as poverty, educational planning, traffic, health, urban sanitation and urban planning as well as environmental protection would all be subjects that require cooperative efforts.

To make progress in these areas and, above all, to gain access to the means necessary to do so, Western monetary and trade policies must be tied more closely together. Our goal should be an Atlantic free trade area that would also include Japan. A new international currency system would be a primary and inevitable step. The first stage in this development could be achieved in Europe through the realization of the planned economic and currency union. Further joint progress could be coordinated through a close coupling of the institutions of the Common Market with those of the United States.

A new formulation of the strategy of flexible response as well as a new division of the burdens of the common defense is required. In view of radically different strategic conditions, the strategy of NATO must be reformulated so that in the future as in the past flexible response can be given in proportion to the political and military factors involved in a given challenge. This process will involve the establishing of a second pillar of atomic deterrence in Europe: a European atomic force in which the nuclear potentials of Great Britain and France continue to develop in close cooperation with the United States. An appropriate effort in conventional military terms on the part of all Alliance partners and especially a satisfactory agreement on the stationing of American troops in Europe are also a necessary part of the same process. Arrangements for the stationing of these troops must be made on a long-term basis. This would also mean that the German-American agreements on the balancing of foreign exchange funds would run for periods longer than two years in duration. To gain a necessary view of the means that are called for and of a just division of the burdens of defense, a European defense budget should be established to provide the basis for a shared Atlantic approach to defense expenditures. The goal of all these efforts must remain the maintenance of a collective defense capability sufficient to resist an attack on Western Europe.

The basic negotiating issues to be taken up in the politics of détente at the ESC and MBFR talks should not be determined separately in various NATO, Common Market, or bilateral talks. They should be coordinated through a joint Western European-American working committee. A series of occasional summit conferences between European statemen and the American President cannot be a substitute for needed ongoing consultation and coordination.

With the achievement of the unification of Europe, the Western world would lay a political foundation that would not only be the most appropriate for maintaining the balance of power in Europe but also the critical balancing factor in the partnership between Western Europe and the United States. The pooling of the military, political, economic, and the intellectual potential of Western Europe could provide the most viable framework for security and détente on the European continent. It could make a decisive contribution to solving the problems of industrial and social development of the Third World and be the basis for a productive partnership between Western democracies.

A European currency and economic union must be realized by the middle of the seventies. Its establishment and further development could be the best basis for the reforms of the international monetary system that must take place to assure healthy development of the Western economic system. Europe itself must create political institutions that will assure its having one representative voice on all questions of foreign and defense policy. In the same sense there should be a unified European policy with regard to aid to the developing countries. All of these would be steps on the basis of which considerations directed towards the political unification of Europe could then take on a more developed form.

This is not an agenda directed against détente but a vital accompaniment to the politics of détente in the framework of Western policy. There is no alternative to the liberal idea that is the basis of the Western world. Americans and Europeans cannot bow courteously to each other, and with a lift of their hats, bid each other "good-bye." Instead, it would make a lot more sense for them to bow courteously to each other, and with a lift of their hats, say to each other, "So nice to see you again."

Acknowledgments

I should like to express my gratitude to my friend Otto A. Kaletsch for his advice and untiring support in making the English language edition of this book possible. I also owe thanks to my colleague Peter Radunski for his help and the preliminary work he did for this book. The U.S. version was translated and edited by Jack C. Voelpel, Otto Krengel and Robert C. A. Sorensen, to all of whom I am deeply grateful.

W. L. K.